Contents

How Kidpower Began 1

How To Start 2

What We Need to Keep in Mind 6

Safety Strategies for Being Out on Your Own 13

How to Set Boundaries with People We Know 41

Suspected Child Abuse 65

What to do About Bullying 71

Working with Different Age Groups 81

Being Advocates for Our Children 83

Helping Children Feel Empowered in the Face of Armed Violence in Schools 86

Sample School Violence and Harrassment Policy 91

Fact Sheet about Kidpower Teenpower Fullpower International 92

Kidpower Educational Materials 95

About the Author 97

Acknowledgements

Kidpower Teenpower Fullpower International safety@kidpower.org www.kidpower.org

How Kidpower Began

How to Teach Self-Protection and Confidence Skills to Young People

The Kidpower Guide for Parents and Teachers

Irene van der Zande
Executive Director/Founder

For local information:
Kidpower of Colorado
www.kidpowerCS.org
coloradosprings@kidpower.org
10 Boulder Crescent, Suite 100
Colorado Springs, CO 80903
719-520-1311

Kidpower Teenpower Fullpower International safety@kidpower.org www.kidpower.org

Copyright and Permission to Use Information

Copyright Notice. *How to Teach Self-Protection and Confidence Skills to Young People: Kidpower Introductory Guide for Parents and Teachers Colorado Edition* Copyright © 1996/ 2008/2012 Irene van der Zande. Licensed to Kidpower Teenpower Fullpower International.

No part of this material may reproduced in any manner without prior written permission of the author except for brief quotations in reviews.

However, a wealth of free articles, videos, podcasts, and other materials are available though our online Library at www.kidpower.org.

Use of Material. Readers are encouraged to use ideas from Kidpower's educational resources to teach "People Safety" skills in their personal and professional lives. We ask that readers follow our Permission to Use Guidelines to ensure proper acknowledgement to Kidpower Teenpower Fullpower International when they use any examples, ideas, stories, language, and practices that they learned from our program and that they let others know how to reach our organization.

Restrictions. Individuals and groups must have an active certification or agreement with Kidpower Teenpower Fullpower International to be authorized to teach, promote, or organize workshops or other presentations using the Kidpower, Teenpower, Fullpower program names, workshop names, reputation or credentials. Please visit the Kidpower web site or call our office for information about our instructor certification and center development programs.

Disclaimer. Each situation and individual is unique and neither the author nor Kidpower can make any guarantee about the safety or effectiveness of the content or techniques described in this book. We do not accept responsibility for any negative consequences from the use or misuse of this information.

Please Note. This book is an introductory version of *The Kidpower Book for Caring Adults: Personal Safety, Self-Protection, Confidence & Advocacy for Young People*, which has 400 pages of comprehensive explanations, step-by-step practices, and inspiring stories. *The Kidpower Book* includes chapters about how to create a foundation of emotional safety for young people as well as how adults can protect children and teens from bullying, sexual abuse, and stranger safety

Publisher. Kidpower Teenpower Fullpower International
P.O. Box 1212, Santa Cruz, CA, 95061, U.S.A; (0) 1-831-426-4407
safety@kidpower.org

*Dedicated with great love to
my husband Ed van der Zande,
for his constant, unwavering support,
and to our daughter Chantal Keeney,
our son Arend van der Zande,
and our granddaughters Svea Corrine Keeney and Ida Mae Keeney,
who are my biggest inspirations for doing this work.*

Drawings are by the children in Judith Martin's special classroom for deaf and hard of hearing children.

Kidpower Teenpower Fullpower International safety@kidpower.org www.kidpower.org

How Kidpower Began

In 1985, in a public bus station, in the middle of the day, a man threatened to kidnap my children. I was with my seven-year-old daughter, six of her friends from school, and my four-year-old son. The man charged towards us with his arms outstretched shouting, *"I'm going to take one of these girls to be my bride!"*

The children clung together in a scared huddle. My little boy was so frightened that he tried to squeeze his body behind his big sister. The people who were standing all around froze. No one came forward to help us. This happened not because they were bad people but because in an emergency, bystanders often go into denial.

I was able to stop the man by doing what most of you readers would do. I put myself in between the man and the kids and I yelled, **"YOU ARE NOT ALLOWED TO SCARE CHILDREN!"**

Later I thought that this was not the most intelligent thing I had ever said in my life, but it was all I could think of at the time.

The man yelled back, *"I can do anything I want! I can say anything I want!"*

We had a face-to-face shouting match. Finally, I ordered a man who was standing close by watching to *"Get over here and help me! Can't you see these kids are scared?"* Embarrassed, the bystander walked over and the man threatening us ran away.

The children were fine. From their point of view, when I yelled, the bad guy ran! But I wasn't fine. The faces of the terrified children, the frozen bystanders, and the image of the contorted attacker were burned into my brain. I kept wondering, "What if he'd knocked me down? What if he'd even touched one of the children?" I knew I'd try to fight him but I didn't know how. I kept imagining the unprotected children who he went on to assault.

I took a full-force self-defense course with a head-to-toe padded instructor and found the skills to protect my children and myself. I knew that I couldn't be with my children all the time, so I joined with other concerned parents, as well as martial artists, educators, public safety officials, and mental health professionals, to create Kidpower.

Kidpower Teenpower Fullpower International is now a charitable nonprofit organization dedicated to protecting people of all ages and abilities from bullying, abuse, kidnapping, and assault through knowledge, action, and skills. Instead of using fear to teaxh kids about violence prevention, Kidpower makes it fun to learn to be safe! Since 1989, Kidpower has served over two million children, teenagers, and adults, including those with special needs, from many cultures around the world, through our educational resources, in-person workshops, and consultation. Our vision is to work together to create cultures of caring, respect, and safety for everyone, everywhere!

How To Start

Understand the Issue

Violence against young people is a major health issue of our time. Emotional and physical violence against children has reached epidemic proportions in our society. The facts are alarming.

Rape crisis center and law enforcement officials estimate that about one in three girls and one in every four to seven boys will be sexually assaulted before the age of eighteen. If a child has a disability, the risk is even greater. Some experts estimate that over 83% of women with developmental delays will be sexually assaulted, almost half of them ten times or more.

According to the U.S. Department of Justice statistics from a 2002 study quoted on the website of the National Center for Missing and Exploited Children[6] (NCMEC):

- 797,500 children (younger than 18) were reported missing in a one-year period of time resulting in an average of 2,185 children being reported missing each day.

- 203,900 children were the victims of family abductions.

- 58,200 children were the victims of non-family abductions.

- 115 children were the victims of "stereotypical" kidnapping. These crimes involve someone the child does not know or a slight acquaintance who holds the child overnight, transports the child 50 miles or more, kills the child, demands ransom, or intends to keep the child permanently.

According to the American Association of University Women, 85% of girls and 76% of boys reported being sexually harassed. Harassment had clearly more detrimental effects for girls—70% of girls (24% of boys) said the experience made them very to somewhat upset.

According to the Department of Justice in a 2008 study, 75% of sexual assaults against children happen with people they know. Of these, over 85% are acquaintances - neighbors, friends, teachers, religious leaders, youth group elders, health care professionals, babysitters, and other children. The rest are family members - parents, siblings, or other relatives. Contrary to popular belief, child molesters do not obviously stand out in society, and most child molesters are equivalent to average residents of U.S. households in terms of education, marital status, religious affliation, and distribution of ethnic groups.

Ellen Bass, co-author of *The Courage To Heal*, which is an internationally best-selling book for adult survivors of childhood sexual abuse, has worked with thousands of people who were abused as children. One significant finding of her work is that even what seems to be a "minor" molestation can leave a damaging, sometimes hidden scar.

Bullying harms millions of young people in the United States as well as throughout the world. A national study of 15,000 schools found that 29.9% percent of students are involved in bullying either as a bully (13.0%), a victim (10.6%) or both a bully and a victim (6.3%). It is reported that one third of middle school students feel unsafe at school because of bullying and do not report such behaviors to school personnel because they are scared, lack the necessary skills for reporting, and feel teachers and administrators do nothing to stop the bullying. Young people who are bullied are at risk of losing their self-confidence, and in extreme cases may commit suicide or become violent.

Face Our Fears

Thinking about statistics like these can be overwhelming. There is nothing more horrifying than the thought that something might happen to the children we love. Before we can be effective in teaching children how to keep themselves safe from danger, we need to deal with our own feelings.

Abduction. Assault. Abuse. When you read these three words, and you think about young people, what feelings come up for you? Across the boundaries of many different countries in many different languages, I have heard people give the same answers. *"Terror . . . Rage . . . Grief . . . Hatred . . . Denial . . . Fear . . . Anger . . . Despair . . . Disgust . . . Revenge . . . Sadness . . ."* I have come to believe that caring adults throughout the world share a huge psychic pool of grief about the terrible things that people sometimes do to children.

We have every right to these feelings. We deserve support for them from other adults. But if we dump our load of upset onto children when we are trying to teach them about personal safety, it's not going to work. Either the children will take in our feelings and become overly fearful, or they will be so turned off that they will go into complete denial and refuse to listen. To avoid feeling overwhelmed, they will put their hands over their ears and say, "I know! I know! I know! I know!"

It helps to remember that children experience their world in a different way than we do. When I took my first self-defense course, I was filled with sorrow at all the tragic stories of so many women who had survived terrible experiences.

After a particularly hard class, I walked into my home to face my darling eight-year-old daughter, Chantal. I gathered my little girl into my arms and burst into tears.

Being used to her emotional mother, Chantal sat calmly on my lap as my tears dripped into her hair and asked, "What's the matter, Mommy?"

"It's just that you're such a wonderful kid," I said sadly, "and I wish I could give you a better world to live in."

"It's all right, Mommy," Chantal said cheerfully. "Look at it *this* way—if we were living in the time of the dinosaurs, we'd *all* have to worry about being eaten, ALL the time!" Suddenly I realized that my fantasy of a safe perfect world for my child was just that – a fantasy – and not her reality at all.

We need to approach the issues of safety with people in the same matter-of-fact manner that we approach safety with water or with cars. We can teach children to swim without going into the gory details of drowning. We can practice holding hands and crossing the street together as we tell children calmly "You know, you have to look both ways before you cross the street, because you might get hit by a car." There is no reason to explain exactly what it's like to have your body smashed to bits by a moving vehicle. We will be most effective if we teach children to be safe with people without giving details about what exactly happens in assault and abuse.

The good news is that most bad situations can be avoided if children know what to do. They can learn to use clear body language, set appropriate boundaries, check and think first before they get close to strangers, protect themselves from bullying, and move away from most trouble before it starts.

No Guarantees

To paraphrase Sir Francis Bacon, a sixteenth century philosopher, "To have a child is to give a hostage to fortune." We cannot completely protect our children from all the bad things that might happen to them. Unless we can accept this reality, we might try to restrict their lives until they end up feeling helpless or resentful.

Our job is to protect children as best we can while helping them learn how to protect themselves. We want them to see life as an adventure, not as a calamity, and to see themselves as adventurers, not as victims of the unexpected.

Children sometimes ask questions like "What if there are too many bad guys for me to get away?" or "What if somebody starts shooting with a big gun?" The underlying question really is, "What if I'm overwhelmed and can't get away?"

We can tell children, "The People Safety skills we are learning work in most situations. Anyone, no matter how careful, no matter how strong, can think of a situation where nothing works. It's just like knowing how to be safe on the street. Even if you do everything right, a drunk driver could drive up onto the sidewalk and hit you. But that almost never happens. You can learn how to keep yourself safe most of the time."

Set a Good Example

One of the best things we can do for our children's safety is to take a self-defense course for ourselves. Children can learn more from what we do than from what we tell them to do. They need to see that we believe that we have the right and the ability to protect ourselves before they will believe that they have the right and the ability to protect themselves.

For a woman, taking a self-defense course can give a whole new meaning to the term "Super Mom." One day I was hiking with my family in the mountains. A large black bear suddenly strolled across the trail. Our children, Arend and Chantal, immediately ran to stand next to me.

My husband, Ed, smiled and asked our kids, "How come you're running over to Mommy?"

"Because," said our son, Arend, who was then five, "if that bear gets too close, then POW! Mommy will stop him!" Chantal nodded.

A little alarmed at their level of confidence, I said, "Daddy knows how to protect you, too. Besides, if we don't bother that bear, it's not going to bother us."

"Maybe," Arend replied. "But we saw what you learned in your class, Mommy. We feel better standing next to you."

Ed smiled at me again. "Hmmm," he said, "I think that this is where real change begins. And the next time we're walking down a dark, lonely street, I'll let YOU go first!"

Using This *Introductory Guide*

This *Guide* includes information for adults as well as ways to discuss safety issues and practice skills with children. Remember that adults need more information about the problems of abuse, assault, and abduction than kids do. Basically, children just need to know what their People Safety rules are and how to follow them. Please error on the side of emotional safety in what you choose to share with children.

All of the stories we tell in Kidpower are true. We have sometimes changed names or details to protect the confidentiality of our students. To avoid pronoun problems, the gender is changed somewhat randomly in our examples.

This *Guide* is for **any** adult who cares about the safety of children. As the reader, the children you are concerned about are **your** children and you are **their** adult.

What We Need to Keep in Mind

Safety and Self Esteem Come First

The underlying Kidpower principle is that:

> *The safety and self-esteem of a child are more important than ANYONE'S embarrassment, inconvenience, or offense — theirs, ours, or any other person's.*

This principle is easy to agree with, but hard to live by. As the reader, do *you* ever dread the possibility of being embarrassed? Do you get upset at the thought of embarrassing others? Do you hate to be interrupted when you're busy? Do you dislike bothering other busy people? Do you worry that people might get mad at you? Do you hate getting angry at others? Do you know children or adults who become overwhelmed if they feel bothered, embarrassed, or angry – or who try hard to avoid bothering, embarrassing or offending others? How do the people you know react when children do things that are embarrassing, inconvenient, or offensive, especially to adults?

Being able to apply the Kidpower Principle in their daily lives will help children to protect their safety and their well-being. We want children to interrupt busy adults if they have a safety problem, even if this seems rude. We want them to set boundaries about unsafe touch, even if someone they care about feels sad. We want children to be loud and assertive when someone is threatening them, even if this is embarrassing.

This means we must avoid giving children contradictory messages. Suppose a kindly neighbor starts to stroke the curly hair of a toddler while she's sitting in her stroller? Imagine that this little girl tries to pull away, but her mother lets the lady keep touching her hair, perhaps even telling her daughter to be more polite. What message is the mother giving her child about her right to stop unwanted touch?

Timothy Dunphy, the other Co-Founder of Kidpower, tells a story about his daughter at age three. "I was leaving for a two week trip. When I tried to kiss my child good-bye, she suddenly decided to say 'No!' I felt really sad about going away for so long without that kiss, and I was tempted to try to coax her into doing what I wanted. But I realized that it was more important for my daughter to know that I would respect her boundaries than it was for me to get that kiss."

Our children will be safer if they believe that we will back them up when they are taking care of themselves.

Belief is the Most Effective Self-Protection Tool We Have

Our belief in ourselves as powerful, valuable, competent people is the most important self-protection tool we have. Kidpower principles and practices are all intended to create understanding and experiences that will help build positive beliefs for children and for adults. We also want to reduce exposure to experiences and information that will take away children's belief in themselves as being strong, capable, and important.

For example, children who are over-exposed to the news often get a terrifying world-view that leaves them feeling powerless. Just as we make choices about much of what our younger children eat and drink, we can keep track of much of what they see, read, and hear about.

Even if we cannot protect our children from hearing about scary events, we can help them put things into perspective. One little boy asked, "What if somebody blew up our school with a bomb?"

His teacher said, "That is not likely to happen."

"But it does happen!" he protested. "The news people on TV talk about bombs and people getting shot almost every day."

"Yes," the teacher answered in a very reassuring voice. "Bad things can happen. And that is very sad and very terrible. But most of our schools are very safe. Even if you hear about scary things on the news, most of the time most people can live safe happy lives."

Accept Your Child's Unique Path

It's hard to resist the temptation to compare children with each other. Yet we know that each child needs acceptance as a unique being who is following a unique path. Our job is to be realistic about what each child most needs to learn. Different ages, different life situations, different family priorities, and different personalities determine how best to build each child's safety and confidence.

Is the child a "super hero" who thinks he's invincible and is likely to lack caution? Is he a shy child who might freeze and be intimidated into going alone with someone? Instead of being anxious, it works best to acknowledge and build on the potential strengths of a child's personality. The child who knows no fear often has a lot of energy and can be very effective at boundary setting. The shy child is often extremely aware of the environment and able to avoid trouble.

Prepare for the Unexpected

If we are startled by the unexpected, adrenalin rushes through our bodies. Often, this flood of adrenalin turns into panic. Panic, in turn, can cause a freeze, flight, or fight response. A deer will stand as if frozen in the headlights of a car. A startled rabbit will flee frantically, sometimes leaping toward the dog chasing it. An injured dog might try to fight and growl or snap at the veterinarian who wants to help. Instead of going into a panic, our children will be safer if they can use their adrenalin to take focused effective action.

Often, we don't recognize potential danger because our minds are on automatic pilot and our bodies are acting out of habit. For example, we might want our children to be kind, friendly, and obedient to most adults in most situations. But it can be a mistake to have this behavior be their automatic habit with all adults all the time everywhere. Instead of being on automatic pilot, we can teach children how to make a habit of paying attention to what is happening, being aware of their different choices, and making safe decisions about what actions to take.

We can prepare children for the unexpected through giving them the chance to practice what to do and how to do it.

Train our Body Memories

In real life, we tend to do what we've practiced. Actually doing something instead of just talking about it creates kinesthetic experiences. These experiences give us memories that we can feel with our bodies as well as think with our minds.

Everything we've ever done is stored inside our brains but we often experience the memory in the nerves and muscles of our bodies. This is often called our "body memory." For example, suppose you imagine right now that I am throwing you a ball. You can probably feel the sensation of catching that ball—or, if you're like me, of trying to catch that ball and missing it. Either way, that feeling is what is meant by a "body memory."

Children who have rehearsed though role-plays how to respond appropriately in different situations are much more likely to do what they've practiced in real life. Many of our students who handled dangerous situations successfully told us later, "I didn't have to worry. My body just seemed to know what to do."

Tell and Then Ask . . . Show and Then Practice

Just telling or showing children what they need to know is not enough. In a study funded by the U.S. Department of Health, *The Safe Child Book* author, Dr. Sherryll Kraizer, tested the ability of over 1,000 elementary school children to act on the safety rules they had been told to follow. Over half of the children agreed to go with a strange adult or to allow an adult to keep pinching their cheeks after they said they didn't like it. When the children were re-taught with an opportunity for each child to rehearse the skills through role-plays, over 90% of the children were able to act in a safe fashion.

The Journal of Consulting and Clinical Psychology (1987) reported a study of kindergarten children where half learned skills through practice and role-plays and the others watched the experimenters role play the material. Results showed that children who practiced themselves were more effective at learning the skills.

One mother told us, "I spent years telling my 10-year-old daughter how to avoid every dangerous situation I could imagine, but when she was approached by someone she felt sorry for, she froze. The Kidpower training helped her work through this experience and gave her the confidence in her body as well as her mind that she would know what to do in the future."

Children usually understand more from what they say and do than from what they see and hear. They tend to be very literal and to have different ideas than adults do about how the world works. We can learn a lot by asking children to tell us and show us how they would handle different situations.

Long ago, my son Arend, then aged nine, was home sick from school. As a storm raged outside, Arend watched a child's program on television. Since I had to leave him alone for a short while, I suddenly thought to ask him, "What if the electricity goes out while I'm gone. What would you do?"

"No problem," Arend replied confidently, "I'd just take the batteries out of my flashlight and plug them into the TV to make it work again." Since his creative thinking could have gotten him electrocuted, my son's answer tuned me in that he needed a little more explanation about what was and was not a good plan.

Take the time to coach children to be successful in practicing the skills presented in this Guide. We do not need to be polished actors to play different "Let's pretend" games with our children. The learning of self-protection skills is a basic health and safety issue rather than a matter of choice for the child. Often, children will complain at first. If we are insistent about practicing, they will feel better…and so will we.

Practice makes perfect for any type of skill. A number of years ago, I felt nervous about leaving town. It was just two years after the big earthquake in Santa Cruz. Suddenly, we had a series of small tremors. Before leaving, I needed to reassure myself that, even if my preteen children were alone in the house in an earthquake, they'd be okay. I told them, "Show me what you'd do if an earthquake came."

Chantal and Arend both looked exasperated. "Aw, Mom!" they argued, "Not NOW! We already know all about this."

"Humor me!" I said. "Nothing else is going to happen tonight until you show me what you know. No television. No books. No dessert. Nothing!"

Arend looked mutinous but his big sister advised, "Save your breath. When Mom gets like this, it's faster to give in than to argue."

So we went from room to room in the house. I yelled "Earthquake!" and Chantal and

Arend ran to stand under doorways or crouch under tables. Most of the time, they were right. But in one room of the house, the doorway was next to our gas furnace. I was able to warn my children that this was not a good place to stand in an earthquake. By the time we were done, I was ready to go on my trip with more peace of mind.

Instead of worrying or lecturing, insist that your children tell you and show you what they would do.

Tell the Truth — But Not the Whole Truth

Long ago, the parents of some young children I know were so upset about the world's political situation that they felt compelled to explain to their kids just how bad things might get. It was sad and a little scary to hear their five-year-olds wondering, "Will bad guys wreck the whole world with nuclear bombs before I can grow up?"

When these parents asked what kind of curriculum was going to be included about nuclear and chemical warfare in the first grade, I was relieved to hear the teacher say, "These are just little kids. Let's teach them about the brave people who work for peace — but spare them the horrors of war."

The same principle is true when teaching children about People Safety. Our job is to help our children understand what they need to know to keep themselves safe. Beyond that, it can be harmful to children to raise images that were not there before. It works best to let them set their own pace about what else they are ready to know. Differences in age, personality and life situations make what's appropriate vary tremendously from child to child.

When children ask difficult questions, we need to decide what information will best serve them. We can choose not to answer by changing the subject. We can find out what's in their minds already by asking them what they think. We can just answer the questions without giving detailed explanations.

When Chantal was eight, we sat together watching a children's show on TV. During the commercial, there was a public service announcement for the local rape crisis center. My daughter turned to me with round, innocent gray eyes and asked, "What's rape, Mommy?"

"Oh no!" I thought, hating the idea of shattering her innocence. "Rape," I said, "is a way some people have of hurting other people."

"How do they hurt them?" Chantal demanded.

"By making them have sex when they don't want to," I sighed.

"Isn't sex supposed to be for making babies?" Chantal wondered. "And for grown-ups who are married or really, really in love with each other?"

"Yes," I said, dreading how much more she was going to ask, "but sometimes people who are hurt inside get things all twisted up and they hurt other people all sorts of ways. Rape is one of those ways."

"Oh," my child said, satisfied for the time being. "Thank you. I like knowing the meaning of words. Today in school we learned what photosynthesis means. Do you want me to explain it to you?"

"Sure!" I said, grateful for the reprieve.

Find the Time to Ask . . . and the Patience to Listen

With our hectic lives, it's hard to remember to make room—at least a few minutes every day—to check in with our children. Children are safest if they believe that their adults really do care about everything important to them—the good and the bad, the trivial and the significant. To develop this belief, children need opportunities to answer questions like, "How was your day? . . . What went well for you? . . . What went wrong?"

When our children have problems, it's tempting as adults to jump right in with solutions. Most of us know better. But, if you're like me, it's hard to tolerate our children being unhappy. With our greater life experience, we adults can't help having lots of excellent ideas for what our children should do and how they should feel. Of course, our kids might call our good advice "lecturing," and they might feel judged and pushed and as if we think that they can't figure things out for themselves.

Children will benefit the most from being listened to with interest and without judgment. Usually, our children's unhappy feelings come from causes that require no action or advice on our part. Most of the time, the most helpful thing we can do is to encourage our children to talk while we listen.

Especially as they get older, it's important for our children to believe that we want them to deal with unpleasant feelings rather than ignore them. Keeping our children in the habit of talking about uncomfortable issues can prevent a host of problems in the long run.

Many children will resist doing this. Thinking or talking about upsetting experiences brings up unpleasant feelings. It's understandable that many children would prefer to stop thinking or talking about something that makes them feel bad. They may also lack a language for what happened or feel like it is stupid or their fault. Children need to learn that continuing to talk about problems, even though they may feel worse at first, will help them to feel better in the long run.

One good technique for checking is to ask children every once in a while, "Is there anything that you've been wondering or worrying about that you haven't told me?"

One mother went home after a Parent Night and asked this question of her five-year-old daughter, who we'll call Molly. Molly burst into tears. It turned out that Molly's father's boss's son had been pulling up her skirt. This small child, who was only four, told Molly that he would make her father lose his job if she said anything. With her parents' support and the skills she practiced in class, Molly was able to yell and get help when he tried to bother her at an office picnic a few weeks later.

Mistakes are Part of Learning

Children often become upset when they make mistakes. They think making mistakes makes them bad. Because they don't want to feel bad, they can become trapped into continuing to make the same mistake over and over or into pretending that nothing happened. One of the most important lessons we can teach children – and remember ourselves -- is that mistakes are part of learning.

The shame that comes from hiding mistakes can be destructive to a child's joy in life. We can help our children by being realistic about this. To paraphrase Mark Twain, "Good judgment is the result of experience and experience is all too often the result of poor judgment."

Have you ever made the same mistakes over and over again? I have. This is when I remind myself that we do not have to be perfect to be GREAT!

Safety Strategies for Being Out on Your Own

Be Aware, Take Charge, Get Help

The Kidpower safety strategies are to:

1. Be and Act Aware of what's around us;

2. Take Charge of our safety and well being; and

3. Get Help whenever we need it.

These strategies are based on our understanding of what happens in a predatory attack, often called the Pattern of Attack. The first step in this pattern is **Selection**— an attacker wants to select an easy victim. In one study, convicted felons were shown videotapes of people walking down the street and asked which ones they would choose as victims. They all picked the same people. These criminals said that they were most likely to try to attack people who looked scared, uncertain, or as if they were not paying attention.

The second step in the Pattern of an Attack is **Position**—an attacker seeks to create a position of advantage with respect to a potential victim. An attacker wants privacy, so that other people won't see what's happening and possibly stop the attack or report it. An attacker wants control. This means that the attacker will try to get close to a potential victim and will try to get this person into a more vulnerable position.

To have privacy, an attacker is more likely to approach people who are in more secluded areas of a park, street, or building. To gain control, an attacker will often try to get a potential victim to lower his or her guard by asking an innocent question or offering help. Giving an attacker more privacy and control is like giving more fuel and oxygen to a fire—the problem will almost always get bigger.

The third step is **Domination**—the attacker scares, hurts, humiliates or steals something from the victim.

The fourth step is **Escape**—the attacker tries to get away and not get caught. Usually, the only way police officers can help us is by trying to catch the attacker, but this is after the attack has already happened.

The sooner we can interrupt the pattern of an attack, the safer we are likely to be. This is the reason for the Kidpower Safety Strategies. If we show that we are aware, the attacker will probably decide to leave us alone. We can prevent the attacker from creating a position of advantage if we take charge of our space and our environment.

We can move away, yell, ask for help or fight if we must. Any time we face possible danger, the problem is not over until we <u>get help</u> by telling a supportive person what happened.

Angie's Story

After taking a Kidpower workshop, a student who we'll call "Angie" went with her mother to an indoor shopping mall. She talked her mother into letting her visit the pet store and the bookstore by herself, and they agreed to meet in the snack bar later. While Angie was walking around enjoying being on her own, a very nice man she didn't know said, "Hi!"

Angie said, "Hi!" back. When the man kept walking towards her, she moved away from him to where there were more people.

The man followed her. He came up close and said in a very mean voice, "Shh! Be quiet and come with me and you won't get hurt!"

"NO!" Angie yelled. "THIS IS NOT MY DAD!" The man looked startled and melted back into the crowd.

Angie went up to the cash register in the nearest big store, which is where her mother had told her to go for help if she needed it. When she tried to get the clerk's attention, he said impatiently, "Wait at the end of the line! Can't you see I'm busy?"

"I see you're busy, but I feel scared." Angie said. She told the clerk about the man.

"He's not here anymore. Don't worry about it!" the clerk said.

"My parents shop here all the time and you're going to get in trouble if you don't call the security guard!" Angie said. When the security guards came, Angie described the man. They found him in a deserted part of the mall, bothering a little boy.

Because she understood how to be aware, take charge, and get help, Angie kept herself safe and even protected another child from danger. By teaching the following Kidpower skills, you can help the children in your life learn to do the same.

Acting Aware, Calm, and Confident

The way to stop most attacks before they start is to project an attitude of awareness, calm, and confidence.

There are two kinds of attacks – predatory and competitive. Predatory attackers try to select somebody who seems like an easy target and who acts like a victim. They are most likely to choose people who have their heads and bodies closed down, shuffle their feet, look scared, wander aimlessly as if they don't know where they are going or act as if their head is up in the clouds daydreaming or listening to music.

A lot of people are surprised to hear that aggressive behavior can also provoke an attack. A competitive attack happens when somebody feels challenged or threatened and starts a fight, often out of fear or to save face. Aggressive behavior includes making fists, making sarcastic remarks, staring at somebody, sneering facial expressions, and strutting.

You can explain this to children by saying, "There is a way you can carry yourself in the world that will make it less likely that people will bother you and more likely that people will listen to you. We call this 'acting aware, calm, and confident.' Awareness means 'noticing'—and letting other people know that you notice—what's happening around you. Confidence means 'believing'— acting as if you believe in yourself. Calm means staying in charge of your body and your mind so that you can think clearly and make safe choices for yourself.

People who bother children have told us after they were caught that they were more likely to pick on someone who was not paying attention or who looked easy to scare. It is also important to act calm because attackers say they are more likely to bother people who seem angry and act like they are looking for a fight."

Let children tell you how to use all their senses to be aware. "What can you use your eyes for?. . . Yes, your eyes can help you see if a car is coming. . . What can you use your ears for? . . . Your ears can help you tell if someone is sneaking up behind you. . . What can you use your nose for? . . . Your nose can help you smell if there is a problem like a fire . . . There is also something called 'intuition' or the 'uh oh' feeling. . . Do you know what that is? . . . It's the feeling that you sometimes get in your stomach or the back of your neck or arms that tells you that something is wrong . . . Your intuition or 'uh oh' feeling is like all your other feelings. It is another way for you to be aware of everything that is happening around you."

Remember that the goal of practicing personal safety skills is to build confidence and competence, not to create fear. Look for progress, not perfection. Focus on the skill, not the problems.

Practice showing awareness, calm, and confidence by having children walk across the room with their heads up and their eyes looking around. Make sure they really notice what's behind them and have a confident posture. As they walk, you can coach them to "Take your hands out of your pockets . . . Let your arms swing free at your sides . . . Take big quick regular steps as if you know where you are going . . . Have a calm face. . .Lift your head up . . . Relax your shoulders . . . Look around. "

If a child is visually impaired, she can still turn her face towards an attacker, letting him know that she notices he is there. If a child uses a wheelchair to get around, he can still move away from an attacker with awareness and confidence.

You can have children practice noticing what is going on around them by standing behind them so they have to really look or listen while you do or say something silly for them to report. This helps make the practice fun and interactive.

Being aware works in nature too. *The Smithsonian Atlas of Wild Places* describes a forest preserve in India where 50 to 60 forestry workers a year were being killed by Bengal tigers. The rangers studied how tigers attack workers and tried out an interesting experiment. They had the forestry workers put masks of people's faces on the backs of their heads. Until the tigers figured out that they were being tricked, not one person wearing a mask was attacked. This is because tigers in nature do not like to attack if someone is looking at them!

Feeling ONE Way and ACTING Another

It is an important self-protection skill for children to understand that they can *feel* one way and *act* a different way. If someone is making them uncomfortable or scared, it is normal to *wish* that the problem would go away or to try to pretend that the problem is not there. Instead of wishing or pretending, children are safer if they use their awareness by looking towards the problem and then move away and get to safety. You can show children that the Wishing Technique usually does not work by putting your hands over your own eyes and saying, "Right now, I can't see you. I am going to *wish* that you cannot see me. All of you wish with me. Wish hard. Do you still see me? . . .You do!"

Children might become nervous or angry in a potentially dangerous situation. You can tell them, "It is normal to feel worried or mad on the inside if someone is acting in a scary way. You can be brave even if you feel very upset and not show this person your feelings. If you act calm, aware, and confident no matter how you feel inside, it gives this person the message that you are not going to be easy to bother. The interesting thing is that, if you act as if you are brave, you will often feel less scared."

Moving Out of Reach

One important way to take charge of our safety is to move out of reach from people who might cause problems for us, whether this is a kid who is always bumping into other kids or a person who we don't know. We also are safest if we move out of reach from other possible dangers, like animals that we don't know well.

Children can develop an understanding of what moving out of reach means with this simple practice. Have a child start by standing facing you and gently poke her on the shoulder. Say, "Right now you are in reach because I can poke you. Move back slowly, splitting your awareness to glance behind you so you don't trip on something and then looking back at me to watch where my hand is so I won't poke you."

Very slowly, reach your poking finger towards the child while she backs away from you. Pause and coach her to keep moving if she stops. Keep one foot planted and start reaching forward until your body is completely extended with your poking arm stretched out. Coach the child to move a couple more steps away from you to give herself lots of room.

Tell the child, "I am going to come towards you quickly and you are going to jump back to move out of reach. Ready? …" Lunge towards the child in a playful way, not a scary one. If the child does not jump back, calmly let her practice again.

Next, create a context that puts the moving out of reach skill into a schoolyard situation. Stand in the middle of the room and tell a child, "Imagine that we are at school and I am a kid who pushes other kids at school. If you walk right next to me, what will happen? …That's right, you will get pushed. Now, use your awareness to notice me, the Pushy Kid. Instead of coming close to me, move out of reach by walking around me in a big circle. Be sure to look back when you get past me to make sure that I don't follow you."

As he walks past you, reach towards the child as if you are going to push him. Help him to be successful by pausing if he gets stuck. Coach him to move further away from you if he comes too close.

Moving out of reach makes it harder for someone who might harm you to create a position of advantage. There is an official martial arts term for this highly effective technique – it is called "target denial" and it means "don't be there." Basically, you are denying yourself as a target to an attacker, whether this is someone you do know or someone you don't.

What's a Stranger?

Before it makes sense to teach children about safety with strangers, they need to understand what a stranger is. Many children are confused about the whole idea. If you ask a group of young children, "What's a stranger?" the answers often are, "A stranger . . . is mean . . . will steal you . . . is a man . . . will give you poison candy . . . looks scary." This is sad because it does not serve children to believe that the world is full of dangerous people called "Strangers."

Older kids and adults know to say the words, "A stranger is just someone you don't know and a stranger can look like anybody." In real life though, just knowing the words isn't enough. The problem is that most of us have pictures in our minds of the kinds of strangers we might worry about. We know intellectually that we cannot tell from the outside what someone is really like. Unfortunately, it is hard not to make assumptions about people based on how they look or act.

Once I was home alone with Chantal at age 12 late at night. Suddenly, there was a knock at our front door. "Who is it?" I called through the door.

A very sad woman's voice said, "PLEASE let me come in. I need help."

When I reached to open the door, Chantal slapped my hand off the doorknob and said, "That's a STRANGER, Mom!"

My daughter was right, so I called again, "What do you need? Can I telephone someone for you?"

The woman, who had a lot of problems, wandered over to our neighbor's house. Even with a large group of adults, she became quite threatening. Our neighbors had to call the police to get this woman out of their home and to where she could be helped. Imagine how much fun my twelve-year-old daughter had scolding me with great indignation, "MOM! You go all over the WORLD teaching people that a stranger is just someone you don't know and you were going to break our safety rules because you felt sorry for someone!"

Sometimes people with bad intentions deliberately try to get us to lower our guard. Someone who looks "different" might be very nice on the inside and someone who seems "nice" on the outside might be mean. Since you can't tell just from looking, it is important to follow safety rules.

When is someone a stranger anyway? One father brought his daughter to Kidpower after she told him, "If I met a stranger, Dad, I'd ask his name because then he wouldn't be a stranger anymore!"

Once you think your child understands what a stranger is, try asking, "Are *you* a stranger to anyone?"

Most young children will say "No!"

If they do, then you can ask, "Are there people in this world who don't know you? . . . Even millions of people? . . . of course! . . . and because they don't know you, *you* are a stranger to them and they are strangers to you!"

At an assembly of sixty young school children, I got them to give all the right answers, including agreeing that I was a stranger. Then I pulled out a puppet from the movie, *The Lion King*. "Who is this?" I asked.

'BABY SIMBA!" yelled my sixty enthusiastic students.

"And if I'm with Baby Simba, am I still a stranger?"

"NO!" they all shouted. At that point, the kids and I had the attention of every adult in the room. The students watched raptly while the principal of their school pretended to be a child. She moved out of my reach and walked over to ask her "Mom" to check about me, even though she was tempted because I was having Baby Simba "tell" her, "Please come and play!"

The way to practice is to point out to children all the times that they see strangers – the first day of school, at the park, in the store. Point out that the reason it is okay for them to be with these strangers is because their adults said it was okay. Ask your child sometimes when you are out in public, "Who's a stranger here? Who's someone we know?"

Help your child understand the difference between somebody they really know and somebody who just is familiar that they recognize, such as the mail carrier. Remind children that even if someone is wearing a uniform, that person is still a stranger.

The goal is to have children be aware rather than anxious. So we recommend that you keep telling children that you believe that *most people are good*. This means that most strangers are good. Yes, a few people do bad things, but not very often. Instead of worrying, children can practice a few skills that will keep them safe most of the time.

Together or On Your Own

Be aware that the safety rules are different when children are together with their adults or when they are on their own. To understand how confusing this is, try asking children, "Who is the *only* person who's with you all the time?"

Younger children usually answer, "My mom…my dad…my teacher…my babysitter." They will say this even when none of these people are around. In the world-view of younger children, their important people always seem to be with them. They are surprised to realize that the only person with you all the time is yourself.

When I said this in one school, a little boy protested, "But God is with me all the time!" I agreed. "God is with you all the time in spirit. But when only God is with you, God wants you to follow the safety rules as if you are on your own!"

To practice, ask the child to stand next to you and say, "Let's pretend that you are a kid and I am a Mom. Suppose that we are in the grocery store and you are trying to talk me into buying the marshmallow fudge strawberry breakfast cereal. Are you with me or are you on your own? . . . That's right, you are with me. And if a stranger comes to give you a free sample of this yummy cereal, is it safe to take it if you ask and I say it's okay? . . . You bet!"

Together *On your own*

Next, move to another part of the room and ask," Now let's pretend that you are still looking longingly at that wonderful cereal that your unreasonable mother will not buy and I'm way down the aisle checking out the healthy oatmeal. Am I with you now, or are you on your own? . . . That's right, now you are on your own. And if that stranger were to come to give you another sample, is it safer to take it or to come and check with me first? . . . Yes, you should check first. Because who is the only person who is with you all the time?…That's right—yourself…And who is in charge of keeping you safe?…That's right—you are. Grownups are here to help you, but you are the only person in charge of you all of the time."

Children are safer when they understand that they can take responsibility for their own well-being. The sad truth is that children are sometimes abducted or molested within a few feet of their parents and within seconds. Ask children to tell you when they are together with their adults and when they are on their own in different situations. For example, if the mother is in the house on the telephone and the child is in the front yard…If the father is talking to a friend and the child is playing on the slide at the park…If the teacher is busy with another student and the child is waiting for a ride home from school.

Children often think they are "together" if they are with a group of other children or with a dog. Be clear that you want them to *Check First* with the adult in charge unless they are *sure* that a situation is safe.

For children old enough to go out in public without an adult along, their job is to *Think First*. We want them to assess whether or not there are adults close by who they can ask to help if someone starts bothering them.

To practice with an older child, explain and act out the following situation. "Let's imagine that you are in the shopping mall. The stores are open. There are lots of people walking around. Let's suppose that I'm from the ice cream shop handing out coupons for free ice cream cones to everyone who walks by. Is it safe to take one? . . . Sure . . . Now suppose you are in another part of the mall where there has been some construction. Most stores are closed and very few people are around. If I try to hand you a coupon, is it safer to take the coupon or to say "No thank you" and walk away? . . . That's right. You are safer walking away."

We also tell older children to assess whether the stranger is treating everybody the same or is singling them out to approach.

Make Safety Plans for Everywhere You Go

Many times children panic because they don't know what to do when they feel threatened. Several twelve-year-old boys were waiting in front of a department store in the city for the mother of one of them to pick them up. A gang of older boys drove up and started yelling at them. When the younger boys fled in all directions, the gang beat a couple of them up. If they had had a safety plan in mind, the boys could have stayed together and backed into the big automatic doors of the department store right behind them.

Make safety plans so that your children know how to get help in any place they might find themselves on their own. Safety when a child is in the yard is with the adult in the house. If the adult is not home, Safety might be with a neighbor or inside with the doors locked. Safety when a child is at school might be with the teacher in the classroom or the principal or secretary in the office. Safety when a child is at the shopping mall might be with the cashier in a store. Safety when a child is on the way home might be with a neighbor or in a store. Safety when a child is in the park might be with a secretary or office employee in the office across the street.

Ask children, "What is a safe place if you have a problem?" You might be surprised at their answers. Sometimes kids say, "under the bed" or "in the bushes in my backyard." Once when I was teaching a second grade class, we asked the children where Safety would be if they got separated from their parents at Costco, a huge discount warehouse type store. After much discussion, they said that they would wait for their parents in by the bathrooms, which were in an isolated place in the back of the store. When the teacher and I asked them why, they said that if they needed to go to the bathroom, well then they would be right there! Picking an easy place to go to the bathroom is perfect logic for a seven-year-old!

What we want children to understand is that Safety is where there are safe adults who can help them.

Children need to know how to reach their trusted adults whenever they have a problem or are not sure that a situation is safe. As soon as possible, teach children how to use pay phones, as well as touch-tone, cellular, and rotary phones. Teach them their full name, your full name, their address, and their phone number.

As more and more people are using cell phones, it is important to explain to children that cell phones can be very convenient but do not always work. Cell phones sometimes are out of range or lose their charge. Any safety plan that is based on calling someone on a cell phone should have a backup plan.

Be sure children know how to call 9-1-1. As one mother found out, the only way to be sure is to practice. Her little boy said confidently, "'Course I know, Mommy! If I have a 'mergency, I just call nine one one! . . . The only problem is, I'm not sure what a nine looks like!"

Tell children that it is important to call 9-1-1 in an emergency, or if they have a safety problem and they are alone. Give examples to help children understand what it means to have a safety problem. You can ask, "Do you call 911 if you're mad at your mom? . . . No. . . What if your mom falls down and hurts her leg too bad to move? . . . Yes, that would be an emergency where you could call 911!"

Move Away and Check First Before Letting Strangers Come Close

If a stranger tries to approach a child who is on his own, his safety plan is to move away and Check First as soon as he notices this person, if he has an adult to check with. You can introduce this in a non-scary way by pointing out to younger children, "The safety rule with people you don't know well is the same as with animals – you do not need to be afraid, but you do want to move away so you can ask your grownup whether this person or animal is okay to be close to."

If a child is old enough to be out on her own without an adult to check with, her safety plan is to Think First about whether or not this is a safe situation to let someone she doesn't know get close to her. In some crowded places such as a movie line, a store or a busy sidewalk, it is often impossible *not* to be close to lots of strangers. Tell children who go to public places independently to move out of reach and get help if a stranger starts paying inappropriate attention to them, tries to get physically closer than the situation calls for or makes them even a little uncomfortable.

To practice, tell children to pretend that they are playing in a park. Have another adult pretend to be a parent, adult friend, or other caregiver sitting on the park bench. Have children take turns standing up, moving away and checking first with another adult while you pretend to be a stranger who calls out their names. You can say, "Don't you remember me? I'm a friend of your Dad's!"

Coach children to stand up, move away and explain to their adult, "A stranger knows my name."

Ask their adult to reward the children by saying, "Thank you for checking first!"

When my daughter first did this practice at age eight, she asked, "What if this person really was a friend of my Dad's and I didn't remember and I walked away? Wouldn't that be embarrassing?"

"Well," I asked Chantal. "What's more important, not being embarrassed or following the safety rules?"

"Following the safety rules!" my daughter said. Then she asked for reassurance, "So if I did that, and the person got upset, you'd still hug me, right?"

"Right!" I promised, hugging her right then and there.

Children can develop more understanding by answering the question, "How could a stranger know your name? . . . Right, by hearing your friends talk to you or reading the name on your backpack or seeing it on your shirt." We explain to students that even if someone knows their names, someone that they are not sure they know is still a stranger.

Move Away and Check First Before Talking to Strangers

The safety rule for children <u>eight years of age or younger</u> is to Check First with the adult in charge before talking to strangers when they are on their own. This is because younger children have a hard time remembering that someone they are talking to is still a stranger. "No talking" also means not shaking or nodding their heads or using other body language to convey information.

The safety rule about talking to strangers for children from around <u>age nine and older</u> is that they should not share personal information and that they do not have to talk to strangers when they are on their own. They might choose to say "Hello" to someone or answer a quick question like "What time is it?" In this case, they still need to remember to be ready to move out of reach if need be. Personal information means telling someone your name, where you live or go to school, about your family, how old you are, etc.

To practice, tell children to walk across the floor pretending that they are going through a park, from home to a neighbor's house or someplace else they might be. Say, "Let's imagine I am a stranger."

Move towards each child calling out friendly remarks like, "Hi, don't you know me? You are in my son's class…You aren't scared, are you? . . . I have a little girl just like you…Where do you live? . . . Isn't this your school? My kids go here too . . . Can you help me? I'm lost . . . Do you know what time it is . . . ?" Each child's job is to follow the rules about talking while moving out of reach from the "stranger" and staying aware. Remind children that being out of someone's immediate reach is not a normal conversational distance.

For many children, it is difficult to do this practice correctly the first time. Children are trained to be polite and to answer questions from adults. If they don't get it right the first time, let them practice the skill again with positive encouragement. "You did a great job being aware, now I want you to practice again and this time remember to not to say anything to me, even if I ask you a question."

Move Away and CHECK FIRST Before Taking Anything From A Stranger—Even Your Own Things

Many abductors trick children by approaching them with warmth and kindness. Children can become distracted and forget to move out of the reach of someone who seems to be helpful by trying to hand them something.

The way to practice is to coach children to: 1) stand up as soon as they notice a stranger, 2) move out of reach, and 3) check with the adult in charge. If there is no adult in charge, their safety plan is to leave their things and go where other people are.

Pick an appropriate setting and possession for each child. Have children start by sitting down so that they can practice standing up when they see the "stranger." Set the stage by telling children, "Imagine that you are in your front yard. Safety is with your dad in the house. Pretend that that chair over there is your dad."

Show children that they cannot be out of reach and take something from someone. Pretend to be a stranger for each child to move away from in different situations (in front of the school, at the park, in the front yard and always identify a safe place for the child to go to). As the "stranger," approach each child pretending to offer something that would be precious to that child. Be sure to pick an object or a pet – *not* a person. For example, you could say "Suppose I have your . . . new tiny kitten that you love a lot that wandered over here . . . favorite toy that you left by the sidewalk . . . bike or ball . . . dad's wallet that has money in it you know he needs . . . ."

Without practice, most children have a hard time walking away from their possessions, even in a role play. They are afraid they will get in trouble if they lose something. As adults, we often reinforce this idea unintentionally. How many times do we tell our children, "Don't take anything from strangers — not even your own things," and how many times do we tell them, "Take care of your things!"?

In one classroom, I pretended to be a stranger holding a Game Boy. The little boy I was practicing with came towards me and said, "**Not my Game Boy**!! You did *not* mean these safety rules for my Game Boy!!"

So I asked him, "What's more important? You or your toys?"

He looked thoughtful and said in a wondering voice, "What's more important, me or my toys? Then he laughed and said, "Why, me, of course." Every five minutes during the rest of my presentation, no matter the rest of the class was doing, this child said to himself, "What's more important? Me or my toys?…Why me of course!" And then he'd laugh again. Whatever else he might have learned that day, I figured that this was what he needed to know the most.

CHECK FIRST Before Changing the Plan About Where You Go, What You Do and Who Is With You.

Children are safer when the adults who love them know *where* they are, *who* they are with and *what* they are doing. Emotional safety for their adults also lies in the same knowledge. A child's safety plan is to Check First with the adult in charge before changing their plans, including with people they know.

By making this a firm rule, we can prevent unnecessary trauma. The police chief of a town near where I live told me the following story. A boy was walking home from school. His Dad, who had gotten off work early, pulled up in his car and said, "Son, let's go get some pizza." So off they went to the pizza parlor.

Meanwhile, the boy's mother was waiting for her son to get home from school. When her son didn't show up, she got scared and called her husband at his office. Since he wasn't there, she reported her son as missing to the police. The police made an all-out search of the town until they found the boy around the corner with his Dad eating pizza!

Remember that most abuse happens with people who children know. A potential abuser will often avoid children who are in the habit of telling their adults who they are with and what they are doing.

The way to practice is to coach each child to walk away and say, "I'm going to Check First!" when being pressured to go somewhere. Choose an activity that this child would really like to do.

Start by saying something like, "Suppose I am your neighbor and you know me. You've even been to my house before. So it's okay to talk with me and to be close. But you still need to Check First before you go with me." Then pretend to be the neighbor and coach the child, Joe, to be successful in the following type of role-play:

> Neighbor: "Hi, Joe, how are you doing?"
>
> Joe: "Fine."
>
> Neighbor: "I've just baked the world's best chocolate chip cookies. Come on over to my house and have some while they're still warm!"
>
> Joe: "I need to **Check First**."
>
> Neighbor: "No you don't! I've already called your Mom and she says it's okay!"
>
> Joe (walking away): "I am going to **Check First**."

Some situations are harder. "Suppose you are waiting in front of your school for your Dad to pick you up. Instead of seeing your Dad, you see me. Let's imagine that I'm your Dad's friend from the office." Pretend to be the office friend and to drive up to where the child, Sandra, is standing.

> Office Friend: "Sandra, I have some really bad news for you! Your Dad hurt his leg and needs you to come right away to the hospital. Get in the car!"
>
> Sandra: "I need to have the principal call first."
>
> Office Friend: "There's no time! Hurry up and get in the car!"
>
> Sandra (walks away): "I am going to call first!"

Tell children that even if you really were in the hospital, you would want them to *Check First* before changing the plan.

•

Many families ask about secret code words that someone has to know before the child goes. This might be a good idea, but only if you have an older child who is able to keep secrets. It's easy to trick a code word out of most children. All someone has to do is ask a girl dressed in a yellow shirt, "Your code word is yellow, right?"

"No," she might say. "It's dinosaur."

"Oh, that's right! . . . Dinosaur . . . Dinosaur is our code word . . . Let's go then." Now that she is in a conversation, it will be harder for this girl to move away. It would be safer for her to leave immediately and *Check First* with her adult in charge instead of waiting to figure out whether or not it is safe to go with this person. Some older children can remember the code word, keep it a secret, and use it appropriately. But many can't. Think of how hard a time people have remembering the passwords to their computers.

Parents need to be very clear about which adults their child can go with without checking first. The younger the child, the fewer these people should be. Teachers can reinforce this rule by pointing out that they always tell parents before they take children to places other than school.

The Gray Zone

In many situations, the rules aren't clear. Our goal is to have children check with their adults when they are in doubt. We want them to have a clear plan in mind that agrees with our idea of what they should do. At parties or in neighborhood stores, you may want to acknowledge to your children that they will be close to and even say "Hi" to people who seem like strangers to them. Praise your child for checking with you, even if it seems unnecessary for that particular person.

If your child takes a long trip alone on an airplane or starts to ride the public transit, be very specific about what is and is not OK to say and do with the person who will be sitting in the next seat. Try to discuss this issue in a clear and positive way without being scary. Remember that children need to know what to do, not how and why bad things happen.

The older and more independent a child is, the bigger the gray zone will become. This is why it is so important to keep updating our agreements and safety rules.

The Rules are Different in Emergencies

Fire fighters, rangers, and paramedics have told us that children will hide or run away from them because they are strangers. The following story from Julie's mother is typical. "When Julie was seven, we went camping. Even though our campsite was right next to the bathroom, she made a wrong turn and headed out to the woods by accident. When Julie didn't come right back and I couldn't find her, I was frantic. Thankfully, a ranger told me that he had found my child. Julie hid in the bushes away from him because he was a stranger. He and another ranger had to keep tracking her so that she didn't get further lost in her attempt to stay away from them."

Remember that most strangers are good. If children are having the kind of emergency where they cannot Check First, they should get help, even if this means going with a stranger.

Tell children that when there is an emergency, the first thing to do is to "Ask yourself, 'Can I check First?' The next question is, 'Who is having this emergency, me or someone else?' If you cannot Check First, your safety plan is to Get Help, even from people you don't know. If the person who is having the emergency is someone else, then your safety plan is to Check First. The best way to help that person is to find an adult you trust who can help rather than to try to do it yourself."

Acting out the following emergencies will help make the distinction clear.

Fire: "If your house is on fire and I am a firefighter dressed just like Darth Vader in a special suit that covers my whole body and face to keep smoke out, is it safer to stay in your burning house or to go Get Help with me? . . . (Get Help) . . . If you are outside your house and I am a firefighter who asks you to help put out the fire down the street, is it safer to go or to Check First? . . . (Check First)."

Lost: "If you are lost in the woods and strangers in a rescue party are calling your name, is it safer to go Get Help with them or to stay lost? . . . (Get Help) . . . If I am a stranger and I ask you to help me to find my child who is lost, is it safer to go with me or to Check First? . . . (Check First)."

Hurt: "If you are riding your bicycle and you fall down and break your leg, is it safer to go Get Help in an ambulance full of strange paramedics, or to stay hurt with no help? . . . (Get Help) . . . . If I ask you to come with me to help someone else who is hurt, even someone you love, is it safer to go with me or to Check First? . . . (Check First)."

In one sad situation, a twelve-year-old girl was approached in a large store by a man who was wearing a uniform. He told her he was a security guard and accused her of shoplifting. He ordered the girl to come with him. She was so shocked that she followed him into an isolated part of the store where he molested her. This girl would have been able to prevent having this upsetting experience if she had known not to go with a stranger, even in a uniform, no matter what that person said and to insist on having the checkout cashier call her parents, who were also in the store.

Remind children that "Someone in a uniform is still a stranger, even a police officer. Unless you are having the kind of emergency where you cannot Check First, tell the police officer that your safety plan is to find your adults first or to stay where there are lots of people."

Most law enforcement officials are very committed to child safety and understand that children need to tell their adults before going with anyone. If a police officer approaches children at their door or on the street, children should not try to check the badge to see if this is really a police officer. Instead, even if there is a safety emergency and their adults are not available, children can almost always call 911 to ask if this police officer is really supposed to be trying to come into their home or take them somewhere. For older children, you can remind them to trust their intuition, and if a police officer is making them uncomfortable, it is okay to ask that a different police officer be with them instead.

Yelling

Odd as it may seem for those of us with loud active kids, most children need to practice yelling for help. If something scary happens, many children are likely to freeze unless they've practiced doing something different. Especially as they get older and more self-conscious, young people often become too embarrassed to make a scene even in the face of possible danger.

Being able to use a loud voice instantly, in spite of feeling embarrassed or scared, is an essential self-defense skill. Yelling can attract the attention of others and take away the privacy that an attacker wants. Yelling makes it clear that someone is not going to be an easy victim, which helps take away an attacker's sense of control.

Yelling stops most assaults. Two girls were walking on the sidewalk after school in a nice neighborhood near my house. A man jumped out of a car and grabbed them. They pulled away and ran. He chased them down the street until one girl started yelling. As soon as she yelled, he ran back to his car and drove away.

Often children don't want to practice yelling because it's "silly" or "embarrassing." It helps to acknowledge these feelings and to say that we all feel this way sometimes. Then you can ask, "What's more important? Not being embarrassed or following the safety rules?" Point out that, "If you can yell when you're embarrassed, you'll be able to yell when you're scared."

Be sure you can yell loudly yourself. Showing children that you are capable of yelling in a strong and effective way is really important. My voice used to freeze up when I tried to yell in front of people. I realized that if I wanted my children to be able to yell for help, I had to set a good example by showing them that I could yell, too. We practiced yelling in private places like the car and the beach. Now, any of us can yell if we wish, anywhere, anytime.

It works best to yell deeply from your diaphragm instead of screaming from your throat. You can tell children, "Put your hands on your throat and say '*No*' from there." Have everyone make a little high pitched "No...No...no." Ask, "Does that sound very powerful?" Next, tell children, "Push your voice down to your belly and feel your belly move as you yell as deep loud short 'NO!' . . . Does that sound stronger?"

Tell children, "Adults are used to hearing kids yell a lot when they're playing. Sometimes they don't know if kids need help. This means that kids need to yell in a strong way and sound like they mean it to get adults to pay attention."

Some experts recommend having children yell "FIRE!" because people are more likely to respond. Our experience is that yelling anything is better than yelling nothing. Having to think too much about what to yell can be confusing. We teach children to yell what makes sense to them. They can yell what they mean, "NO!" or "STOP!" They can yell important information, "THIS IS NOT MY FATHER!" or "I'M BEING FOLLOWED BY A LADY WITH BROWN HAIR IN A BLUE CAR WITH LICENSE #____!" Most importantly, children need to be able to yell for what they want, "I NEED HELP!" or "CALL 911!" or "MOM! DAD!"

Stopping An Attack

Any strong resistance—yelling, pulling away, running away, or using a self-defense move, stops most assaults. We teach children to leave if they can. Children can say "NO!" with their bodies along with their voices by making a quick stop sign motion towards the face of the attacker as they yell.

Before teaching the Stop Sign, have children start by getting into what we call a Ready Position. "Stand with your feet together. Now raise the hand you write or throw a ball with (right hand if right-handed; left hand if left-handed). Use that hand to push the leg on the same side back about a step." This should be a strong balanced stance with the legs not too close, not too far apart; not too narrow or too wide, as if you have just stopped walking. "Raise both hands in front of you with your elbows bent and your open hands facing with your palms forward as if you are pushing against a wall." We do not want children to make their hands into fists because this will send the message that they are looking for a fight.

To make a Stop Sign, have children push their strong hand out towards the face of the person bothering them while yelling "NO!" loudly. Next, they should pull their arm back closer to their bodies instead of leaving it out to get grabbed.

The following story shows how the Stop Sign works in nature too. There was a man who studied great white sharks. He had a theory that if he made a sudden motion towards a shark, it would swim away. His friend said, "What a great idea! You go out in

The Shark Game

the ocean and test it, and I'll stay inside the shark cage and videotape." That's just what they did. Each time a shark came towards the man, he made a sudden motion with his hand towards the shark's face, and the shark swam away. This story shows that even something as fierce as a shark is likely to leave you alone if you don't act like a victim.

Of course, we tell children that in real life, if they see a shark when they are swimming, their safest plan is to move away and get out of the water.

A fun way to practice the Stop Sign is by making a game out of this story. Have one child be the Shark and the other be the Diver. The Shark "swims" towards the Diver who is in Ready Position. As soon as the Shark comes close, the Diver does a Stop Sign with a loud "NO" and the Shark moves away. Switch so that each child gets a turn.

A more realistic way to practice is to pretend to be a scary person who the child yells at and runs away from. It's enough to say general things in a pretend scary way, like "Come here!" or "Get in this car!" or "Do what I say!" **It is NOT emotionally safe to put terrifying thoughts in a child's mind like, "You'll never see your parents again!"**

Give each child something to react to by lunging and yelling. Keep the child successful by not coming too close and by stopping if need be to coach the child through the practice.

The child's job is to yell "NO!" while making a Stop Sign and then to run to a place or person you have agreed is Safety, while yelling "I need help!"

Even very young children can learn this skill. As one aunt told us, "I taught my three-year-old niece to make a stop sign and yell 'NO!' if she felt scared. A couple of days later, a goose started to chase her in the park. When she used her stop sign, the goose ran away! My niece was so thrilled that she challenged all the geese in the park!"

A police officer had a more serious story about her three-year old daughter, who we'll call Beth. One day, Beth ran into the next aisle in the store. A strange man, as a very bad joke, grabbed her arm and said, 'You are so cute! I'll take you away and you'll never see your mother or father again!"
Instead of freezing or bursting into tears, Beth did just what she'd practiced in the Kidpower Parent/Child Workshop. She pulled away, made a Stop Sign with her hand, yelled, "NO!" and ran to her mother and grandmother.

This startled the man who complained, "Your little girl scared me!"

Beth's grandmother, who had not been to the workshop, started to tell Beth to, "Say that you're sorry to the nice man."

She was interrupted by Beth's mother, who told Beth, 'You did the right thing!" and got the man to apologize. Instead of being terrified by the experience, Beth was proud of herself.

Getting Help in Public

When children need help and we are not there, they may need to ask a stranger for help. A child who is lost or bothered by someone in a store needs to be able to get the attention of the sales clerk or security guard, who is probably a stranger. If the child cannot figure out who else to ask for help, the safest choice is almost always to ask a woman with children.

In order to get help, the child will have to talk to the stranger and will not be able to stay out of reach. However, the child should still stay in the public place agreed upon for the safety plan with his or her parent, teacher, or other caregiver.

The first time a child talks to a cashier should not be when that child is lost. Younger children can practice talking to real cashiers by buying things. Start out by standing right with your child to buy something together. Work up to watching as your child walks away from you up to the counter to buy something.

For little people, whose heads are often below the counter, it can be challenging to get the attention of busy adults. Most of us have seen children wait and wait, hoping to be noticed, and then walk away sadly or burst into tears. In many stores, a child will need to walk around the counter to get close to the cashier.

Each time you go to a new place with children, review their safety plan for how to get help if they are lost or bothered. The first thing we want children to do if they think they are lost is to stand tall like the trunk of a tree and look around to see if they can find the adults they came with. If they get worried, they can yell for their grownups. If that doesn't work, then they can find the cashier.

To practice, pretend to be the cashier in the store, who is busy with other customers and coach the child through the following role-play.

> Cashier (talking to another "customer"): "What is it you wanted to buy?"
> Child (clasps the cashier's arm firmly and interrupts with a strong voice): "Excuse me, I need your help. I'm lost."
>
> Cashier (very impatiently and not listening): "I'm busy now, you'll have to wait at the end of the line."
>
> Child (persistently): "But I'm lost!"
>
> Cashier (kindly takes child's hand): "Oh, you're lost! Well, come with me to the manager's office."
>
> Child: "But I'm supposed to wait at the checkout stand when I'm lost."
>
> Cashier (impatient again): "It's the rule! You *have* to come with me!"
>
> Child (pulls away): "NO!! MOM!!! (or DAD!!!)"

We point out that if a child yells "MOM!" or "DAD!!!" in a crowded store, all the moms and dads will turn around. Tell children the cashier can help them without having to take them into the back of the store or away from people.

Older children need to know how to persist in getting help if someone bothers them when they are out on their own. To practice, coach children to get someone's attention, be very clear about what is happening and what they want, and persist in the face of hostility or impatience. Situations could be on a bus, in a store, at the mall, or in a park. For example, you can say, "Suppose somebody made you uncomfortable on the street and I am a worker at the store your parents told you to go to for help."

>Child: "Excuse me, I need help. That person is bothering me."

>Worker: "Him? He's harmless. Don't hang around the store if you're not going to buy something."

>Child: "I see you're busy, but I feel scared. Please call the security guard."

>Worker: "You kids make things up all the time. Go away!"

>Child: " "My parents will be mad at this store and you will get in trouble unless you help me."

>Worker: "Okay! Okay! I'll call!"

Knowing how to persist really does make a difference. After taking Kidpower, one boy was at a roller blade park with his friend. An older boy on a bike kicked him. He immediately thought, "Where is safety?" and went to the recreation kiosk. At first, the recreation worker did not want to get involved. He dragged her to the doorway just in time to see two boys on bikes trying to rob his friend. When the recreation worker shouted, the boys took off, and his friend was safe.

Home Alone

Children need to know our rules about answering the door themselves, even when we're home. If we are not able to hear or see what's happening, we might as well not be there. Once, when I was taking a shower, my son, then aged 4, invited a woman I barely knew into the house. She had come to drop off some work papers. Arend graciously chatted with her and even gave her a glass of water. As I got out of the shower, wrapped in a towel with dripping wet hair, I was startled to see the two of them at my kitchen table.

Unless children are sure that someone is okay to let in, their safety rule is to check with their adults before they open the door. At the same time, it can be scary, especially if we are not there, for a child stand silently listening to someone knock and wait outside the door. Also, someone who is thinking about robbery might knock on the door or ring the doorbell to make sure no one is home.

Whether we are home or not, our children are safer if they do not admit to being home alone or to our being out of reach in a place like the shower. Instead, they can say, "My Mom is busy.' or "My Dad can't come to the door right now."

Practice by pretending to be a delivery person dropping off a package, a florist delivering flowers, someone from the office bringing important papers, an electrician saying that she was told to fix a dangerous wire, or a police officer saying that he needs to check the house. Remind children that even people wearing uniforms are still strangers.

> Stranger (knocks): "Knock! Knock! Hello! I'm here to fix the water heater."
>
> Child (answering from behind the closed door): "Hello."
>
> Stranger: "Get your parents."
>
> Child: "They can't come to the door right now. They're busy."
>
> Stranger: "Please open the door. I'm running late."
>
> Child: "You'll have to come back later."
>
> Stranger: "Are you home alone?"
>
> Child: "No, my parents are busy." (If you haven't done so already, this would be a good time to explain that following the safety rules is even more important than telling the truth.)
>
> Stranger (walking away): "Well, they're not going to like it when they get my bill."

Children who answer the telephone at home can practice not answering questions and not giving personal information to people who call. Make sure they also know you want them to lie if necessary in order not to tell someone they are home alone. Children can be upset by prank or obscene telephone calls. If someone on the telephone starts making them uncomfortable, tell them that they should hang up, even in the middle of a sentence.

Television is Just Pretend

I will never forget my second visit to a first grade classroom shortly after we started Kidpower. One little boy had clearly been thinking about strangers. With big round eyes and a hushed voice, he riveted the classroom with this question. "What if a stranger made himself look *exactly* like my Mom? What if he got clothes like my Mom and a car like my Mom? What if I got in the car 'cuz I thought he was my Mom? And then, when he drove the car away, he peeled the face off?!!!"

"You saw that on television!" I said, wondering how on earth how I was going to keep my promise to the teacher that teaching Kidpower would not scare her students.

"*Yes*!" he gasped, and all his classmates gasped with him. "I saw it with my own eyes—on television!"

"The television camera tricked you." I said, and tried to explain about switching people and trick photography. (This was in the days before digital technology, which is even more confusing to younger children.) The whole first grade looked doubtful.

Thankfully, the teacher threw the full weight of her authority behind me. "Irene is right!" she said firmly. "And the television is wrong!"

Television and movies are a big part of children's lives and shape how they view the world. Children have told us that they learned from television that a magic stone could keep them safe and that one karate chop would level a horde of bad guys. Even in homes where parents restrict watching, children are influenced by what they see at a friend's house or what a friend tells them. Sit down with your child and point out the ways in which television tricks us into believing things that are just not true.

When watching television and movies with your children, take the opportunity to discuss different situations and what the characters could do to protect themselves better. The media is still too full of images of women passively accepting an assault. We can ask children, "Do you think it was a good idea for that woman to go over to that man when he called her? What else could she have done?"

Changing the Plan

Children need to be prepared to change their plan in order to stay safe. If someone is breaking the safety rules, their job is to move away from that person and to go where there is someone who can help them. At school, children can change their plan by stepping out of line if someone is pushing them and going to the back of the line. They can change their plan by noticing when a child or an adult is getting angry and staying away until that person calms down. Out in public, children can change their plan by going into a store instead of letting a stranger who makes them uncomfortable get close to them.

Self-Defense Techniques

Often, young people won't use self-defense to protect themselves because they don't want to get in trouble. Have a frank discussion with children about when it is okay to hurt somebody to stop that person from hurting you. Self-defense training of the kind Kidpower and other organizations offer can increase your child's safety skills and confidence.

In Kidpower, we teach children from about age 6 and older a variety of techniques for breaking away from an attacker. Our students first promise to use these techniques only when they are in danger and they cannot get help. Each of these techniques is done against a target while yelling. In our full-force programs, the targets are the head-to-toe padded instructors. They pretend to attack the students so that our students can deliver full-force self-defense blows to get away. However, it is possible to practice even with a kick pad or sofa cushion. Be careful when practicing to avoid injury to yourself or the child.

Techniques we teach if an attacker grabs a child from the front include:

- pulling away with force;
- jabbing the eyes by putting fingers together like a "chicken beak;"
- hitting the face or throat with the heel of the palm of the hand;
- kicking the groin;
- kneeing the groin.

Techniques we teach if an attacker grabs a child from behind include:

- stomping on the instep of the foot;
- using a fist to hammer the groin;
- jabbing the stomach with a low elbow;
- jabbing the neck or head with a high elbow.

If a child is pushed to the ground, the first thing we want children to do is jump up and run to safety. Techniques that can help a child have time to escape include:

- Stomping up into the groin;
- Stomping up at the head.

We show children that the same techniques and targets can work whether you are on your feet, picked up in the air or lying on the ground.

What about Weapons?

Sometimes adults don't want to talk about weapons with children because it just seems too terrifying. The mystique in our culture about the power of knives and guns can leave us feeling helpless at even the thought of a weapon. It is sadly common to hear stories like that of the two girls who were kidnapped and sexually assaulted near their school by a man who told them he had a gun, even though they never saw it.

The presence of weapons does make an attack more dangerous, but by no means hopeless. The biggest danger is believing the myth that there is no hope. Weapons are by far the most dangerous in the hands of another child or teen, who may have no real idea of the consequences of their use. If a child sees another young person with a knife or a gun, the best thing to do is to leave as soon as possible. Even if a child hears another child or teen bragging about a weapon, it's safer to leave. Lie if necessary. And get help by telling a trustworthy adult.

We can be truthful about weapons without being hopeless. We can say, "If someone has a weapon—a knife or a gun or a club—it would be really scary and you might get hurt. But almost always you can be safe if you remember a few things. First of all, most of the time at the beginning of an attack, someone who has a weapon does not plan to use it. The weapon is being used to scare you into doing what the attacker wants. If the attacker wants to steal something like your money or candy or property, give it away. You are more important than your stuff."

"But if the attacker tries to do something that would make things more dangerous for you, like take you away or tie you up or hurt you, you are almost always safer if you yell and run and fight the best you know how in order to get away. Probably the attacker is not going to use the weapon. One girl was walking home from school and a man pulled up in a car. He pointed a gun at her and told her to get in the car. Instead, she yelled and ran and she was safe."

"You might be wondering, what if the attacker did shoot the gun? Then what? Well, what you see on TV and in the movies, where somebody shoots and everybody drops down dead is just make believe. Most of the time, even trained police officers, even at close range, miss a target moving away from them, most of the time. So the safest thing for you to do is to run away to a safer place as fast as you can."

What About Multiple Attackers or Gangs?

Depending on where they live or what they've overheard or seen on television, even very young children sometimes ask, "What if there are lots of them?" or "What if there's a gang?" Point out that, "If you see a group of people who look like trouble, the first thing to try to do is to go somewhere safe and get help. If you can't, try to calm the situation down. Let them know you know they're there, but don't stare at them. Look towards people with 'soft eyes' -- this means seeing them without making direct eye contact. Let them steal your stuff. Let them say mean things without answering back. It's okay to lie and agree with everything they say if they tell you to. If you think they want to hurt you, though, it is almost always safest to try to get away. Try to run, yell, hit, and kick to get away if you have to."

What if Nothing Works?

What we teach works most of the time. Children need to know that once in a great while there are situations where anyone—no matter how big and strong and skilled they are—could be overwhelmed. Talking about this possibility actually relieves most children. The right kind of discussion can put boundaries around the topic. Children worry most when they think that something is so awful that their adults won't talk about it.

You can say very matter-of-factly, "If you can't get away at first, it does not mean that you did anything bad. It just means that you had bad luck. If somebody does something to make you feel bad, it does not mean that *you* are bad. Do not believe what a kidnapper says to you. No matter what happens, your adults will always love you and always want you and always look for you, no matter what. So you need to keep looking for other chances to get away—like using the telephone or calling out to someone. This situation is such a big emergency that you should run to *any* stranger for help as soon as you get the chance."

Children like the story about one boy who was taken away to a hotel room. The kidnapper made the boy promise not to move while he went to the bathroom. The boy got on the telephone and dialed 911. Even though the boy didn't know where he was, a computer at the emergency center gave the police the address. They got there in time to arrest the attacker before he got out of the bathroom!

The message to keep on trying until you get away is a powerful one. In one news story that we do *not* recommend telling children, a little girl was kidnapped and shackled to the gear shift in the car. When the kidnapper stopped to get gas, this girl used his key to unlock the shackle and ran out of the car and into a truck. She was able to give enough of a description that this man, who had killed other children, was caught. By not giving up, this little girl saved her own life and the lives of other children that this man would have probably gone on to assault.

Being Safe in Our Imaginations

We need to feel safe in our minds—and to have our children feel safe. It can be possible to make ourselves more and more scared by imagining horrible scenes where nothing can work. If you find yourself or your child worrying, ask, "What if this did happen?

How can we use what we know to get out of that situation—or to stop it from ever happening in the first place?" Tell your children that you think it's important that they feel safe inside their imaginations, and to talk to you if they can't stop themselves from worrying.

One little boy said, "What if there were no safe place?"

His friend asked, "Where would that be?"

He thought a bit and said, "On the moon maybe?"

In an indignant voice, his friend replied, "And how likely is that?!"

Sometimes children want details that create pictures they don't need to deal with. Curious children can be very persistent about asking questions we don't want to answer like, "What *exactly* do bad guys do to hurt you or make you feel bad?"

If we think a child might already have heard something awful or have had a bad experience, we can ask, "What do *you* think?" or "Is there something that you want to tell me?" If not, we can say, "I don't want to talk about the bad things that might happen, but probably won't. Doing this just makes us miserable when we don't need to be. I want to talk about how you can keep yourself safe."

How to Set Boundaries with People We Know

What are Boundaries?

A boundary defines a limit. Some boundaries we can *see* – like walls, lines in sports, and crosswalks. Personal boundaries are often invisible but we can *feel* when they are crossed. For example, suppose that I am joking with friends and suddenly someone says something that hurts my feelings. My feeling of "Hey, that isn't funny, that's rude!" is a sign to me that my personal boundary was crossed.

The function of personal boundaries is to protect and contain. Suppose I have a yappy little dog that I keep in my yard inside a fence. The fence contains my little dog so she won't go out into the street and bite people's ankles. The fence also protects my little dog so that she is not hit by a car. The fence creates a personal boundary for my dog. Understanding about personal boundaries can protect us from the intrusions of others and help us contain our own impulses to cross into the boundaries of the people around us.

Kidpower has four principals, or ideas, about boundaries with people we know:

1. *We each belong to ourselves*. You belong to you and I belong to me. This means that your body belongs to you and so does your time, your feelings, and your thoughts – ALL of you! This means that other people belong to themselves too.

2. ***Some things are not a choice***. This is true for adults as well as kids. Otherwise, it'd be no problem next time we go out to drive on the opposite side of the street! Especially for kids, touch for health and safety is often not a choice.

3. ***Problems should not be secrets***. Anything that bothers you, me, or anybody else should not have to be a secret, even if telling makes someone upset or embarrassed.

4. ***Keep telling until you get help***. When you have a problem, find an adult you trust, and keep on telling until you get the help you need.

When he was about eight, my son used to like to say, "Mom, my body belongs to me and I do not have to take a bath!"

I'd say, "Arend, your body does belong to you, but some things are not a choice so you *must* take a bath!"

He'd grump, "I'll tell!"

And I would say calmly, "Go ahead. Tell the whole world that your mother made you take a bath!"

Well, that was fine. Some things are not a choice. But what if I'd said, "Oh Arend, please don't tell! That would be too embarrassing!"? Problems should not have to be secrets and even as Arend's mother, if I had said that, I would have been making a mistake.

More on Problems Should NOT Have to be Secrets

Children from wonderful families often tell me about important issues for them that they think their parents don't care about. I listen, assure them that their parents do want to know, and figure out how they can help their parents to understand. Sometimes we enlist the help of the teacher or a school counselor in talking to the parents with the child.

One eight-year-old girl wept as she described her terror about a neighbor who had said that he would kill her cat because it kept escaping from her house. When she tried to talk to them, her parents had told her not to say rude things about the neighbors.

It can be hard to know when a child is serious. A boy about nine told me that he was having nightmares every night and felt watched all the time. After a steady diet of the science fiction he loved, he couldn't get out of his mind a deep belief that aliens were watching him and getting ready to steal him. He said that his parents told him he had a really great imagination, and laughed when he tried to explain that he really was afraid.

An older girl said that she had very mixed feelings about spending the night at her best friend's house. She loved seeing her friend, but the situation at her friend's home had become very uncomfortable. The parents were fighting with each other so much that her best friend was hanging out with another girl who had gotten into a gang and was using drugs. She was afraid that if she told her parents, they wouldn't let her see her best friend at all anymore.

Quite innocently, many families give very mixed messages about what is and is not okay to talk about. It's safer to have one simple rule—*anything* that bothers any of us should not have to be a secret.

Secrecy is the biggest reason why some abusers can get away with molesting many different children over a long period of time. Children need to know that they should always tell if a person touches or talks to them in a way they don't like, gives them presents or asks them to keep anything a secret. Children should keep telling until someone helps them. Not keeping secrets is the first line of defense against abuse.

What is Abuse?

The word "abuse" has become used so widely that we need to make a distinction between behavior that is experienced by someone as abusive and behavior that constitutes actual abuse.

The truth is that we have all said or done things that other people have experienced as abusive. And we have all had other people say or do things that we have felt to be abusive. Often this happens with our nearest and dearest, because we are around each other so much. Any intrusion by someone else into the boundaries of our personal space, time, bodies, feelings, and spirits can seem abusive.

Physical therapists tell us that their child clients sometimes yell, "You are abusing me!" when they are just doing their jobs. This is why it is so important to acknowledge to children that some things, especially for their health or safety, are not a choice. Professionals use the term "abuse" to describe behavior that is damaging to another person. Adults and children can be harmed by strangers, acquaintances, close friends, and family members. This harm can take many different forms, including:

- physical abuse—hitting, kicking, pushing, crowding, pinching.

- sexual abuse—sexual touching, sexual language, showing or taking sexual photographs or videotapes, sexualizing of a child (comments on a child's sexuality or private body parts, asking or sharing details of sexual experiences).

- emotional abuse—mean teasing, threatening, mimicking, belittling, name-calling, shunning, objectifying (treating someone as an object rather than a person with rights).

Any of these experiences can be damaging to a child. Sexual abuse can be particularly destructive because our society adds the burden of secrecy and shame to this crime. Survivors often feel for years that what happened was somehow their fault.

Adults who were molested as children say that the abuse they experienced became a destructive force that shaped their lives. This is true even if the abuse took place only one time when they were very young or even if they don't remember what happened. The damage can continue until they get help and learn to heal themselves. Survivors say, "I felt completely alone . . . betrayed . . . It was so awful that I made myself forget in order to function . . . I couldn't form healthy relationships and didn't know why . . . I have eating disorders . . . abuse alcohol and drugs . . . am afraid for my own children."

Some Facts About Child Molesters

There are some unpleasant facts about child molesters that we need to know as adults, but that we do *not* recommend telling children. You can give your children valuable and effective skills without telling them the graphic details of how awful things might be. Sadly, the person most likely to hurt or molest a child is someone that that child knows and cares about. Many people who molest children will put themselves in situations where they have easy access to young people. That's why we hear in the media about situations in day care centers and youth groups. That's why pedophiles are seeking relationships with children through the Internet via their computers.

Child molesters sometimes wait as long as two years while they win the love and trust of a family system, a school, or a religious institution before they make their first move. The language they use for this is "cruising and grooming." They groom a child by building a strong emotional connection while testing a child's boundaries with low level touch or intrusions before making an actual overt sexual move.

One of our Centers was asked to do a class in an elementary school where a 72-year-old grandfather was a long-time volunteer assistant in the classroom. He had molested seven children in the classroom while there were teachers and other volunteers in the room without them realizing what was going on. He had been a well-loved member of the school community for years, and the incidents were a shock to everyone.

There are whole organizations of abusers who believe that adults have the "right" to have sex with children and children have the "right" to have sex with adults. Through magazines, and now the Internet, they trade ideas for how to gain credibility and lower boundaries.

Many abusers persuade themselves that the child wants the sexual contact. They are usually seductive rather than overpowering in their approach. They look for children who they think have poor boundaries. The reality is that, because of the power difference between adults and children, most young people without training such as Kidpower will have trouble resisting the psychological manipulation of a perpetrator. Child molesters sometimes say things to make their victims feel at fault and sometimes threaten harm if they tell.

It can be confusing if we tell children to set boundaries with people they really care about by explaining about "good touch" or "bad touch." Sexual touch often does feel good to children at first, and they may not know when their boundaries are being violated. If we call some kinds of touch "bad," children who are molested or who touch themselves are likely to believe that they are "bad." Believing one is a bad person can lead to a host of other problems. Also, we don't want our message to be that sexual touch or attention is always bad for adults. At the same time, as adults, we know that it's not safe for children to be used for sexual purposes.

We can prepare children to protect themselves from sexual abuse by teaching them how to set boundaries around other kinds of unwanted behavior including affection and touch. They will need our support especially in setting boundaries with people they care about the most—with family, teachers, other children, and even with their best friends.

Do Children Really Sexually Abuse Other Children?

Children might molest other children because of power struggles, curiosity, or boredom. They might also be acting out abuse they have seen or experienced directly. Recent studies have documented that children as young as four-years-old have deliberately sexually abused other children. There are many reasons why children do this. Sometimes it is because they have found that this is a powerful way to get attention. Sometimes they are curious and have not yet learned to see and respect other people's boundaries. Sometimes they were abused themselves and haven't gotten help.

Often, children who have been abused look and act like "victims." They give clear signals that something is wrong in their lives. Occasionally, abused children who have not received help might so thoroughly integrate the abuse that they take on the role of perpetrators. They may be very charming, fun to be with, and attractive. They may manipulate other children in the same way that they were manipulated. They may copy as best they can the sexual molestation that was done to them.

What Does This Mean for Me and The Children Important to Me?

As hard as it is to accept, adults need to be aware that *anyone* could become a danger to any child. Even pillars of society. Even kind and loving people. We need to realize that even a child who has been a safe person to be with for years might start to behave unsafely as a result of changing and growing or as a result of having had a bad experience.

At the same time, we don't want children to have to live in continual fear. We want children to be able to play happily with their friends. We want children to feel safe with many different people in many different places. We don't want them to have to see potential danger in every person they know. Living this way would take away their joy in life—and ours.

Adults can best protect children by paying attention and by listening to them. We need to notice and take action when the people around children act in ways that are uncomfortable to us. We should pay particular attention to relationships where there is a strong power imbalance, either emotionally or physically. We can teach children to notice what feels good to them and what doesn't, and to speak up about it. They need to be able to do this with people they love and with people whose approval is important to them. We can be good role models for children through how we set boundaries to take care of ourselves, and through how we support them in setting their boundaries.

Touch and Teasing for Affection or Play Should Be the Choice of Both People, Safe, and Allowed by the Adults in Charge

When my daughter was a toddler, I took her to visit my grandmother in a home for elders. Chantal charmed her great grandmother and all the other folks living there with her happy smile. She even chased a ball that her great grandmother threw for her. All was well until the manager suddenly pinched her cheeks. Chantal burst into tears.

"I know all about babies. She's just overtired. This didn't hurt her!" the manager said, and tried to pinch Chantal's cheeks again! He meant no harm and both he and my grandmother were not pleased with me when I stepped in and stopped him.

Often, people do not realize when children experience their behavior as invasive. They want to connect physically with children, but their cheek pinching, tickling, too tight hugs, and too sloppy kisses are uncomfortable—not fun. Their feelings can get really hurt when you or your children say, "Please don't." It can help to point out to well-meaning adults that affection is not really affection unless it is truly the child's choice.

At the same time, children need affection and often love to play physically. It is very sad to hear grandparents and teachers say that they are afraid to be affectionate physically because they don't want someone to get the wrong idea. It can be hard when the rules about what is and is not appropriate seem to be constantly changing. Instead of not touching or playing with a child, the key is to be clear that affection and play have to be okay both with the child and with other person. A child should have the chance to say, "No" and to have that boundary respected.

It is normal for children to explore and test boundaries. Sometimes children try to play or tease in ways that are not okay with others or that are not acceptable to their adults. They might want to tickle or roughhouse when the other person does not. They might want to play in ways that are unsafe such as climbing on the fence overlooking a cliff or sticking peas into their noses. They might want to play games with their private areas that are against their family's rules. They might want to lean on each other in the middle of class instead of listening to the teacher. Even if two children both really want to and are very careful, their adults will probably not allow them to cut each other's hair. Children need guidance so they can learn to accept other people's boundaries as well as being able to set their own.

You can introduce the idea by asking children, "You know that your bodies belong to you. But most people have been touched in a way that they didn't like. Have you ever not liked it when someone pushed you or grabbed your arm or hugged you too tight or messed up your hair or held your hand? If you like this kind of touch, is it OK?…Yes, of course! But who gets to choose if someone touches or teases you for play or affection?… That's right — touch for play or affection has to be okay with both you and with the other person. Touch, teasing and other kinds of play also have to be safe and allowed by your adults in charge."

What about Being Polite?

Kidpower recommends against pushing younger children to be friendly in social settings. It's just too hard for younger children to understand the difference between polite friendliness and a forced display of affection. When younger children feel comfortable, their friendliness will almost always come naturally.

Older children can be taught to greet people with a handshake and a polite, "It's nice to meet you," or "Hello." They can say good-bye with a handshake and a "Thank you for having me here," or "Thank you for coming." Let them practice what to say while looking someone in the eyes and speaking in a firm clear voice. The effect can be very respectful and acknowledging.

It is reasonable to expect older children to be respectful in social settings with our friends, family, work associates, and neighbors. However, it is another matter entirely to force children to show affection through a kiss or a hug. Children have the right not to like the same people we do. They also may like or love someone, but still not want to show these feelings in a physical way. Forcing children to act affectionate gives them a very contradictory message about their right to set boundaries with people they know.

What About Problems that Come Up During Normal Play?

The fact is that children will engage in activities with each other that might be harmful to one or both of them. It doesn't mean that children are bad people when they do these things. It does mean that our job as adults is to put a stop to inappropriate or potentially dangerous behavior. We can set these limits in ways that respect the child's feelings and are not attacking.

For example, suppose we see a couple of children taking off their clothes and starting to examine each other's genitals. It can be damaging to children if we react in a negative or upset way about this. My husband still winces when he remembers his parents' horror and punishment of an incident that happened when he was only four-years-old. In the game of playing doctor, he let a little girl take off his clothes. His parents were shocked to find them checking out the very interesting ways in which their bodies were different.

Most likely, children playing games like this are just curious. At the same time, we don't want to let potentially sexual behavior continue. Even if both children seem to be okay with what's happening at the moment, there is a possibility that one child is doing this not solely out of free choice, but at least partly to please the other child. Afterwards, a child who went along with a friend might well feel upset about what happened. Even adults often have a hard time figuring out when showing sexual interest is really okay with each other!

We can stop the behavior in a clear and calm way by saying something like, "I can see you're curious about each other's bodies. It's good to be curious, but playing games where you touch each other's private areas is not allowed. If you want to know more about people's bodies, let's talk about it or look at a book."

Similarly, if we see children engage in other forms of potentially inappropriate behavior, we can accept their feelings and set limits on their actions without attacking them. For example, "I see that your feelings are hurt. I want you to talk about what you feel instead of pushing and calling names." Or, "I see that you are really mad that I won't let you climb the ladder because it's not safe. You can disagree with me and be angry but you may not climb the ladder and you may not hit me."

What if a Child Asks, "Why Not?"

Children are bombarded with innuendo, language, and images that are sexual, violent, dangerous, and mean. They see things on television, share extensive information with each other, and notice much more of what adults say and do than we can possibly imagine. They may well be puzzled about why we want to put a stop to their copying what they see and hear all around them.

For behavior that is acceptable neither for adults or kids, we can say, "Yes, I know some friends have families that make a lot of putdown jokes. And I know that's how people often talk on television or in movies. But in our house, the rule is that we speak to each other with respect." Or, "Yes, I know that daring each other to eat cockroaches is what they do on television. But people in our school are not allowed to try to pressure each other to do things that are disgusting or dangerous."

It is important to model being responsible for our actions if we break our own rules about inappropriate behavior. We can teach our children a great deal about being honest if we are willing to say things like, "I'm really sorry for losing my temper and screaming. I don't want you to scream at each other or at me. This means that, even when I am tired from working all day and annoyed because you glued newspapers all over the table, I am going to do my best not to scream at you. Now, let's clean up that table!"

For sexual behavior, all we really need to explain is, "Using this kind of language or playing games that copy this kind of behavior is not safe for kids to do. It is something that grown-ups can do, but not kids." It is no surprise to children that grown-ups get to do lots of things they can't.

Safety Rules About Touching Private Areas

Showing affection is great. But adults should be aware of the impact that seeing overt sexual behavior can have on children. Children notice what is happening on the television and in the room. Many parents ask what they should do when their children are the ones who are being sexual. Sexual exploration by young children is very normal. They need clear guidance about what our rules are. You can say something like, "People's vaginas, penises, bottoms, and breasts are private areas. These are the parts of your body that are covered by a bathing suit. For play or teasing, it is against our safety rules for other people to touch your private areas. It is also against our safety rules if other people ask you to touch their private areas or show you pictures or videos of people touching anyone's private areas."

We don't want children to feel that there is something shameful about their bodies. Families have very different standards about what is and is not okay regarding children touching their own private areas when they are by themselves. It is important that you decide on your rules in a way that fits your values. As one mother said, "My preschooler is just fascinated with his penis. Whenever I read to him, he starts playing with himself! I keep having to tell him, 'If you want to play with your penis, you need to be by yourself in your room. Doing that is private. If you want me to keep reading, you need to stop!' He leans against me and sighs, 'Oh, all right! Now please don't stop the story!'"

Sometimes children will explore what the boundaries are by touching us inappropriately or by asking inappropriate questions about our sex life. We can move their hands or bodies away from us gently. We can refuse to discuss a topic by saying matter-of-factly, "That's private."

Very few children will be able to resist asking the universal question, "Why?"

And we can give them the universal answer, "It just is."

Some Things Are Not a Choice

Let's be honest. Lots of times children have to put up with unwanted touch just because the adults in charge say so. If they run into the street, we'll grab them if we can. We'll hold their bodies to stop them from hitting or throwing. If they won't do it themselves, we'll make them sit in a car seat, wear their seat belts, put their shoes on, or leave the park when it's time to go—physically if need be.

To avoid confusion, be clear that unwanted touch and loss of privacy for health and safety are *not* choices for children. A teacher may help a young child go to the bathroom. A nurse or doctor may examine a child's genitals or give a shot. Encourage children to discuss these events to help remind them that touch or loss of privacy, even for health and safety, are not secrets.

Some forms of sexual abuse are disguised as being necessary for health reasons. If children know that things that bother them should never have to be a secret, and are able to tell someone, they can get help if they need to. If what is being done to them is necessary, there is only good and no harm in having everyone involved in the habit of openly discussing everything.

We can acknowledge our children's right to dislike something while informing them that it is not their choice. One boy aged ten told his father, "My teacher was abusive to me today."

His father put his instant anxiety about the teacher aside, took a big breath, and asked calmly, "What happened?"

"Well," his son complained, 'She made me stay in at recess because I forgot to do my homework."

His father put his instant indignation at his son aside, took another deep breath, and managed to stay calm. "I understand that you hate missing recess and were really angry. And, if you don't bring your homework to school, your teacher is doing her job to make you finish it there . . . Now how can we help you remember your homework?"

Protecting Yourself from Hurting Words

Many times children are tormented or coerced into feeling bad about themselves, getting into fights or making what they know are unsafe choices because they react to the words that other people say to them. How many times do adults have the same experiences? Learning to have power over words can keep words from having power over you!

To introduce the issue, you can ask children, "How many of you have had your feelings hurt by something mean someone said to you? . . .Things like 'I hate you!' or 'You're stupid!' or 'You're ugly!' or 'You're not trying hard enough!' How many of you have been told to 'just ignore it?' How many of you have still felt bad even when you tried your best to ignore what the person said?" Most children (and adults too if we're honest) will keep raising their hands.

If we don't protect ourselves from the mean things people sometimes say, those words can end up stuck in our minds or our hearts and they can stay with us for a really long time. But we don't have to let that happen. We can use our own thoughts to protect ourselves from hurtful words.

One useful image is to imagine putting hurting words into a trash can instead of taking them into our hearts or minds. In my many years of self-defense work, this is the technique I personally use the most!

We can do this with a real trash can. Some classrooms where we've done classes even have small trash cans with a sign that says "Put your hurting words here." Children are told to use their hands to catch the hurting words that someone says to them and then they walk over to the trash can to throw the mean words away. Children even sometimes will walk over to the trash can and yell their own mean words into it instead of saying them to someone else.

Our most famous technique is the Kidpower trash can. Put a hand on one of your hips. The hole made by your arm is the top of your trash can. When people say mean things to you, you can catch these words with your hand and then throw them into the trash. This technique works even better if you replace the mean words by saying something nice to yourself.

For children, doing something active like using or imagining a trash can works much better than being told to "Just ignore what people say to you." After the Kidpower program has been in a school, teachers tell us they see younger kids on the playground, hands on their hips, throwing away words like "I don't like you!" and saying, "I like myself!"

Older children like the image, but might resist practicing because it seems too childish. We can acknowledge their reality by saying, "Of course you won't do it like this out in the school yard. But practicing with me will help you be able to use the trash can as a metaphor, or a picture for your mind, when you need to. You can say something positive to yourself silently instead of out loud."

To practice, tell children that you are going to say some mean things that are not true so they can practice throwing them away. **Be clear that you are just pretending so that the children can practice**. Pick words that children are already dealing with rather than giving them new ideas about hurtful things to say.

> Adult: "If I say, 'You're stupid!' you can throw those words in your trash can and say, 'I'm smart!' ....Ready? ... You're stupid!"

Child (catching and throwing mean words away): "I'm smart!"

Adult: "If I say, 'I hate you, you can say, 'I love myself!' . . . Ready? . . . I hate you!'"

Child (catching and throwing mean words away): "I love myself!'"

Other common attacks and affirmations include:

Attack: "You're ugly!"

Affirmation: "I have my own way of looking good!" or "I look great!"

Attack: "How could you make such an awful mistake!?"

Affirmation: "Mistakes are part of learning!" or, with a shrug, "Nobody's perfect!"

Attack: "You have such dumb shoes . . . clothes . . . hair!"

Affirmation: "I like them!"

Attack (to a child with glasses): "Four eyes!"

Affirmation: "I like my glasses. They help me see!"

Attack: "You're awful because you're different!"

Affirmation: "I like the way I am!" Or, "I don't have to be perfect to be great!" Or, "I am proud of who I am."

You can let children pick out words they want to throw away. You can notice language that bothers them and use that. Just because something seems silly to us doesn't mean that it won't really bother the child. One fourteen-year-old boy was mortified because, since he was growing tall so quickly, other kids were calling him "long spaghetti." These words had become so loaded for him that he had to watch the Kidpower staff practice with each other before he could practice for himself. His parents said later that just doing this simple exercise changed his whole attitude about going to school.

The ten-year-old daughter of one of our instructors arrived home upset every day. When she rode the school bus, other kids kept calling her "tree stump" because she was short. She felt too old to use the trash can the way she'd practiced, but just using her imagination wasn't enough. So she and her mother invented a mini-trash can that she could use behind her back so the other kids wouldn't see it.

The next day, the girl came flying into the house shouting, "It worked! It worked! When they called me 'tree stump,' I made my mini-trash can. The kids asked me what I was doing, and I told them I was putting their words into my mini-trash can. They got so interested that they forgot all about teasing me."

To make a mini-trash can, curl up the fingers of one hand against your palm to make a hole and use your thumb to push words into the top of the hole.

Without permission from parents or schools, we never use foul language in Kidpower children's programs. Instead we tell children, "I want you to think of the *worst* words you can think of for someone to call you . . . *do not* say these words out loud . . . When I say, 'You're nothing but a Really Bad Word,' you can imagine that I said the words you were thinking of. Throw those words away! Then say, 'I like myself!'"

Sometimes children and adults too have a certain word or phrase that really bothers them. Often these words involve foul language that adults normally forbid children to use. It can be very effective to let children practice out loud with language that upsets them in order to take the power out of these words.

Using the garbage can

Taking in Good Words

It can be just as hard and even more important to take in the good things that people say to us than it is to keep out the bad things. Suppose someone tells you, "You look great today!" Do you squirm and say something like, "Oh, but I didn't get enough sleep . . . and I pulled this old shirt out of the closet . . . and . . . !"? Suppose someone says, "You did a great job on this project!" How likely are you to say, "Oh but here are ten things wrong with it!"?

The nice things that people say are compliments! We don't want to throw compliments in the trash! We want to use the good things people say to help us build our belief in ourselves. Even if you have no trouble with compliments, how true is this of many people you know? Given these examples, it's not surprising that many children need to be taught how to accept compliments graciously. You can practice by having children look you in the eye, take the compliments you give into their hearts and say, "Thank you!"

Our goal is to take in the positive and keep out the negative. A useful image is the semi-permeable membrane. You can explain to children that, "Our bodies are made up of billions of tiny building blocks called cells. Each cell is surrounded by an amazing surface called a semi-permeable membrane that lets in the food and oxygen that our cells need to live. This membrane also keeps out the poison and pushes out the waste. If our cells didn't have that semi-permeable membrane, they would die. We can imagine having the same kind of membrane working like a filter to help protect our spirit. "

Because this idea is a little complicated, it can be helpful to children to say, "Would you eat rotten food? . . . Of course not! Where does rotten food go? . . . Into the trash (or the compost bin). . . Right, that's where rotten mean horrible words should go too! And what about good food? . . . Good food helps us grow strong and so do good words. So does it make sense to throw good words and compliments into the trash? . . .No, you want to take good words into your heart."

Controlling What We Say to Ourselves

You can tell children, "We all have a voice inside our heads that talks to us all the time. Sometimes this voice says nice things, sometimes it says hurtful things, and sometimes it just makes observations. If you're not sure what I mean, it's the voice right now inside your head that's asking, '**What** is she (or he) talking about?' When this voice says nice things to us, we should listen. If this voice is mean, we should throw those bad thoughts away just like we throw away the hurtful things that other people say."

For adults, as well as kids, learning to control what we say to ourselves will reduce a lot of unnecessary hurt in our lives. For example, how often do you look at yourself in the mirror in the morning and say to yourself, "I do not like the way I look!" Imagine being able to throw that thought into your trash can while you tell yourself, "I have my own kind of beauty!" Or, "I have my own way of looking good."

Have you ever winced with embarrassment at a memory and said to yourself, "I can't believe I said or did that!" How about telling yourself, "Mistakes are part of learning!"

When you are learning something new, do you ever feel discouraged and sigh, "This is too hard! Everybody understands this but me! I'll never get it right!" You can replace that thought with the message, "I just need to give myself more time to learn!"

Timothy tells a story about how his daughter said sadly on her way to school, "Dad, my inner voice just told me that I'm stupid because I forgot to do my homework." Then she brightened up and added enthusiastically, "But my *other* inner voice says that it's okay because I can do my homework at recess!"

Stopping Unwanted Touch

If children can stop *any* kind of unwanted touch, they will be able to stop most forms of sexual abuse. It can be tempting to have a sexual undertone for the sake of realism when practicing these boundary-setting skills. But it is important to avoid this temptation, because there is no need, and doing this could be emotionally dangerous for the child. The unwanted touch can be a gentle pat to the arm, stroking hair, a gentle shove, holding hands, or hugging.

"Please take off your hand."

You can start by reminding children that, if they like this touch it's okay, and that it's also okay to change their minds. Parents sometimes worry that this kind of practice will stop their children from wanting to be touched. This reaction is possible, but not likely. Of the thousands of children we have trained through Kidpower, we have had not one report of a child becoming less affectionate! What we do have are hundreds of reports of children feeling empowered because they know that they have a choice.

The Kidpower levels of intrusion are based on what molesters try to do, but are also true for all sorts of other violations. From a personal perspective, the levels of intrusion happen when another person:

• Doesn't Notice that I don't like what he or she is doing.

• Doesn't Listen when I say, "Stop."

• Makes Me Wrong by getting upset because I said, "No."

• Breaks the Safety Rules by offering bribes or threatening me to try to get me to do something.

• Makes Me Promise Not to Tell by making threats or pleading with me.

The Kidpower method for introducing and practicing the different levels of intrusion

Doesn't notice

and appropriate responses is described below and in the drawings.

Doesn't Notice Intrusion: Explain to children that, "Most of the time when people bother us, it's because they just don't notice that we don't like it." To practice, touch the child gently as described above, perhaps, for example, by rubbing Carol's foot. Acknowledge that, "If you like this, it's okay. But let's suppose that you changed your mind."

Doesn't Notice Response: Coach Carol to look you in the eyes, use her body to move your hand away, and say politely, "Please stop rubbing my foot." It's important to coach Carol to use a "regular voice" that is neither whiny nor sharp. Most of the time, just giving someone a clear message with our eyes, words, and body is enough.

Doesn't Listen Intrusion: One of my favorite things to do is to ask a room full of children, "Have you ever noticed that sometimes other people don't listen to you?" Of course, they all shout, "Yes!" To practice, rub Carol's foot again and say something like, "But this is fun!" or "But you always let me do this!" or "Come on, you know you like this!"

Doesn't Listen Response: Carol stands up, takes two steps *away* from you while facing you, makes a boundary with her hands and says very firmly but still politely, "I said please stop rubbing my foot! I don't like it!" If someone doesn't listen, our job is to send a stronger message. To make a boundary, have Carol extend her arms in front of her, palms open, to create a barrier (or fence) between herself and the intruder.

Doesn't listen

Makes Me Wrong Intrusion: People might get embarrassed or upset when we tell them that we don't like something they do. Sometimes they try to make us feel bad for telling them to stop. To practice, look upset and make comments such as, "But Carol, don't you like me?" Or, "You're being rude." Or, "I thought you were my friend," Or, "You're hurting my feelings." Or, "Can't you take a joke?" You can add, "If you cared about me, Carol, you'd let me rub your foot."

Makes Me Wrong Response: Carol says, "I really like you and I don't want to hurt your feelings, but I just don't want you to rub my foot." Or, more simply, "Sorry and please stop!" When we tell children that they can put these two thoughts together—wanting to please someone and still not wanting that person to do something—it's as if we gave them a piece of gold! Some children like being able to add, "Our family's safety rules are that I don't have to be touched if I don't want to be."

Breaks Safety Rules Intrusion: Tell children, "If a person tries to do something which will leave you feeling bad inside, this is against our safety rules. One way of breaking the safety rules is by offering an unsafe bribe. A bribe is like a trade where someone gives you something in exchange for something from you. A safe bribe is something everyone knows about and is not going to cause you to break your safety rules. An unsafe bribe is when someone tries to give you something or do you a favor to get you to do something that you know is wrong or unsafe or will get you in trouble. And we know from experience that if you accept an unsafe bribe, you will end up feeling bad inside." To practice bribery, pick something that might be precious to Carol, "I'll give you a kitten . . . ice cream . . . a trip to Disneyland . . . if you'll just let me rub your foot!"

Makes me wrong

Breaks the safety rules

Breaks Safety Rules Response: Carol stands up, backs up, makes a boundary with her hands and says in a strong loud voice, ***"Stop or I'll tell!"*** As an alternative, older children can say, "Stop or I'll leave!" They can simply decide to leave as they say, "It's time for me to go now." Tell children, "Even if the person

"Stop or 'I'll tell!'"

does stop, it's still important to tell an adult you trust anytime anyone does something that makes you uncomfortable."

<u>Other Ways of Breaking the Safety Rules Explanation and Practice</u>: Give examples of different situations where we want children to say, ***"Stop or I'll tell!"*** For example, another way of breaking the safety rules is through a misuse of power. To practice, look stern and say something like, "I'm bigger than you, so you have to do what I say!" Or, "I'm the adult and you're the kid. You *have* to obey me even if you think it's wrong!"

Tell children that people also sometimes break the safety rules by breaking the rules about touching someone's private areas. Reassure children that of course you would never do that to practice!

Remind them that the safety rule is, "For play or teasing, other people are not to touch the private parts of your body—these are the parts covered by a bathing suit—nor are they to ask you to touch their private parts or show you pictures of people touching their private areas. If you get the uncomfortable feeling that someone even *might* be about to break this safety rule, then right away you say, 'Stop or I'll tell!'"

To practice, coach children to say, "Stop or I'll tell!" after you say, "This touch is about being a grown-up," or "Let's keep this touch a secret." Kidpower instructors *never* use sexually explicit language or gestures while practicing with children unless parents have specifically asked for this practice because of special circumstances. Even then, we are very careful. We want children to be successful in stopping abuse, not to

Makes me promise not to tell

experience what we do as abusive.

<u>Makes Me Promise Not to Tell Intrusion</u>: As an introduction, have all the children present stand up, make their boundaries with their hands, back up, and shout, "STOP OR I'LL TELL!" Frown, glare at them and in a mean voice say, "You'd better not tell. Something really bad will happen to you if you tell!"

Next, very calmly ask the children, "If someone did that, would it be scary? . . . Well, this is a time when you can lie and break a promise to someone because you are going to say, 'Okay, I won't tell if you stop!' and then what are you going to do? . . . TELL! . . . Most of the time we want you to tell the truth and to keep your promises. The reason it's okay to lie and break a promise is because you are doing it to be safe and because you are going to tell an adult you trust as soon as you can."

To practice, threaten, "You'd better promise me not to tell—or you'll be sorry!" Or plead, "Look, I could lose my job if you tell. Please, please don't say anything. Promise?" Notice that the threats are general, not specific. Our goal is to build skills, not fear.

<u>Makes Me Promise Not to Tell Response</u>: Carol says, "Okay, I won't tell if you stop!"

Then ask Carol, "And once you're away from the person, what will you do?"

Carol says, "I'll tell!"

About Lying and Breaking Promises

Many parents express concern at the thought of teaching their children to lie and break promises. After all, we work very hard to teach our children to be honest and to keep their commitments. We want them to care about other people.

Child molesters take advantage of our children's wish to be honest, honorable and kind. They have many ways of coercing children into agreeing not to tell. Also, if someone is making threats or pleading about telling, it can be dangerous for a child to keep saying, "I'm going to tell! I'm going to tell!" It's important that they feel able to say what someone wants them to say in order to get out of the situation safely. Children need our specific permission that it is okay to lie and break a promise as long as they are doing it to be safe and as long as they come and tell an adult they trust about what happened as soon as they can.

About Telling

Some studies show that it takes an average of two years before children report being abused. If the adult they talk to reacts in an upset way, children are very likely to withdraw the story. This means that children need to know who to tell and how to tell.

Start by asking children, "Who are some adults you could tell if you had a problem?"

Common answers are, "My mom . . . my dad . . . my grandma . . . my grandpa . . . my aunt . . . my uncle . . . my teacher . . . my principal . . . my counselor . . . my minister . . . my rabbi . . . my big brother . . . my big sister . . . the police . . . the fire department . . . my dog."

"Your dog?"

"My dog's an adult and listens to me all the time!"

"It's great to tell your dog, but be sure to tell a human adult as well!"

After a child decides who to tell, the next job is to make sure that the adult being told hears and understands. This isn't always easy. When my sister was seven, she had a long conversation with my father as he was reading the newspaper. My mother asked my father, "Do you know what you agreed to?" My astonished father learned that he had just promised that we could be the lucky home for one of the chicks about to be hatched in her second grade classroom! To their credit, my parents kept their commitment. Silky was a grand addition to our family for many years.

A child's failure to get our attention usually doesn't work out that happily. Too many times, the reason children don't tell their parents about something bad happening to them is because they think that their parents already know. Sometimes children think that we can read their minds. Sometimes they did tell us and we didn't hear them. Sometimes even though we heard them, we didn't understand what they meant. The solution is to teach them to persist in telling the whole story until they get the help they need.

To practice, let the child decide who they are going to tell and how that person might be busy. Pretend to be that person being very, very involved in—talking on the telephone, watching a football game on television, working on the computer, meeting a deadline for work, getting the checkbook balanced, reading a murder mystery and being just about to find out who did it, getting dinner ready when it's very, very late. Have the child persist even though you act oblivious at first and then grumpy as in the following example with eight-year-old Steve:

> Steve: "Dad, can I talk to you?"
>
> Oblivious Dad (reading): "Go ahead, Steve. I'm listening."
>
> Steve: "Today at school some kids pushed me into the bathroom and locked the door."
>
> Oblivious Dad (still reading): "Mmm . . . hmmm . . . that's nice . . . glad you had a good day, Steve." (Try asking children, "Do your parents ever say, 'Mmm . . . hmmm . . . that's nice' when they aren't listening?" Most of them will laugh and say, "Yes!")

Steve (clasping Dad's arm): "***Dad**! Look at me! I need your attention.*"

Annoyed Dad (in a loud voice with a big frown): "***Steve**!!! **What**!!! **Can't I have a moment's peace**?*" (Ask children, "Do your parents ever get grumpy if you interrupt them when they're busy? . . . Should Steve keep telling his Dad anyway?")

Steve: "But Dad, this is about Kidpower!" Or, "This is about my safety!" (Many families agree that saying "It's about Kidpower" will be their signal for a problem about safety or well-being.)

Very interested Dad: "Oh, about Kidpower. Why don't you tell me what happened?"

Steve: "Billy pushed me today."

Annoyed Dad: "You interrupted me for *that*! You and Billy push each other all the time! I'm too busy right now for this nonsense!" (Ask children, "Did Steve tell Dad the whole story? . . . Can Dad read Steve's mind?")

Steve: "But this time Billy was with a bunch of kids and they pushed me into the bathroom and it was smelly and dark in there and I felt scared and embarrassed."

Understanding Dad: "Oh, I'm so glad you interrupted me! That does sound upsetting! I'm sorry that I yelled at you. Let's talk this over and figure out what to do."

Another situation to practice is one in which the adult doesn't believe the child and says things like, "You must have misunderstood . . . Uncle John was just trying to be friendly . . . You're making this up . . . You're overreacting . . . Jane's one of our best camp counselors. Work it out with her!" The child's job is to think of who else to tell and to keep telling until someone does something about it.

Be sure your children know how to get hold of you or someone else they trust, no matter where they are. They need to know how to get out of uncomfortable situations. Be clear that they have the right to call on the telephone—even in the middle of the night—even from school or camp or someone's house. Make sure that the people who care for your children know that you expect them to help your children get in touch with you if they want to.

Remind children, "Touch should not be a secret. Favors should not be a secret. Presents should not be a secret. And, of course, problems should not be a secret."

Why Kids Don't Want to Tell

Especially as children get older, it doesn't always work to say, "Just tell me what's bothering you." Often, they really don't want to.

Common reasons young people give for not telling their parents about their problems are: "I'm afraid they'll get upset or give me a lecture." Or, "They *always* overreact!" Or, "They never do anything anyway." Or, "Somebody will get back at me." Or, "I broke too many rules to tell." Or, "I want to be grown-up enough to handle things myself." Or, "I don't want to be disloyal to my friends." Or, "I'm afraid my parents will make me stop seeing my friend if they find out, and that person is important to me."

Start by acknowledging children's reasons for not wanting to tell. We can then enlist their help in finding strategies for overcoming the resistance created by these reasons.

If we want children to talk to us, our most important job when they come to us is to take a breath and do our best to stay calm, no matter how upsetting the subject is.

When it comes to issues of safety and well-being, no matter *what* children say, the first comment out of our mouths needs to be a matter-of-fact positive statement like, "I'm glad you told me."

This can be very hard to do. But if we want children to come to us with their problems, we need to be safe people to come to. What children need from their adults first and most of all is to know that we will listen. After we have listened and fully understood their point of view, then we can take whatever action seems appropriate.

Different Situations

Once children have the basic skills of boundary setting, you can use role-plays to have children practice stopping unwanted touch or other behavior in a wide variety of situations. Many of the following experiences are fine as long as it's okay with the child, but the child needs practice to stop someone when it doesn't feel okay to the child, or when it could be dangerous.

- an uncle at a family wedding ruffles the child's hair.

- a soccer coach shoves the child playfully.

- a swim teacher manipulates the child's body to get ready to dive.

- a family member pinches the child's cheeks.

- a babysitter hugs the child too tightly or too long.

- a family friend who is supposed to drive the child home arrives drunk.

- a family friend pulls the child onto his lap.

- a piano teacher leans over the child and holds the child's hands in the correct position on the piano keys.

- a neighbor gets so angry when the child breaks a vase that she starts grabbing the child's arm and calling the child names.

- a neighbor with a new camera says, "I'd like to take your picture. Why don't you go put on a bathing suit?"

- a teacher keeps a child in at recess and holds the child's hand.

- an older kid at school tries to get the child to use drugs.

- an older friend tries to borrow money.

- a parent's work associate alone with the older child in the office makes suggestive remarks ("You're getting to be such a woman — I really like the way your body is changing").

- a babysitter insists on trying to help an older child get on her or his pajamas.

- a camp counselor takes a child alone on a walk and puts an arm around the child's shoulder.

If someone wants to give children help they don't need or that makes them uncomfortable, they can say, "Just show me." Or, "I can do it myself." If someone is angry and out-of control, children can often calm things down by saying very politely, over and over if necessary, "I'm sorry I made that mistake. I'll do my best to fix it. Please don't yell at me, please don't grab me, and please don't call me names."

Live What We Teach

We have to be willing to speak up for our children when they come to us complaining about unwanted touch or attention. This can be extremely difficult with members of our family. However, we can tell our family members and ourselves that if our children can set boundaries with the people close to them,

This is what happens if you don't stop someone from pinching your cheeks.

they will be far more prepared to stop potential molesters.

In one evening class with parents of toddlers, Paul's mother asked, "What if the child seems to like it sometimes and hate it other times? My husband plays tickling games with our two-year-old son. Sometimes Paul says 'No!' and then says 'More!'"

I said, "It's important for Paul to learn that his words have power. He will get the idea if your husband stops when Paul says 'No' and continues when Paul says, 'More' or 'Yes.'"

Paul's mother said, "But my husband loves this game! He tickles Paul every night as part of getting him ready for bed. It's one of the only ways he knows how to interact with our son. But sometimes Paul really seems to hate being tickled."

I asked, "If Paul can't stop his father from touching him in a way he hates, how is he going to stop someone else?"

With a look of horror dawning on her face, Paul's mother got up and said, "You know, I would never let my husband tickle me the way he's tickling our son. And he hated being tickled by his older brothers. It was almost a kind of torture. I'm sorry to walk out on your talk, but I've got to go home right now and tell my husband about this. It's almost time for him to put Paul to bed!"

Suspected Child Abuse

How Will I Know?

Every time another story hits the news, it's normal for caring adults to worry and to wonder, "How will I know if my child is being abused?" It's important to stay aware of the possibility of child abuse without jumping to conclusions. Many of the symptoms for what might be caused by abuse could also be symptoms of other problems.

No matter how okay we make it for our children to talk with us, they may face an experience that shocks them so much that they can't. They may show stress in subtle ways, such as becoming extra clingy or trying extra hard to please. They may express their unhappiness in ways that upset us such as suddenly doing poorly in school or being destructive or starting to lie.

Ask questions when your child seems uncomfortable. Pay attention to comments like, "I don't want to go visit ___ anymore," or "I keep having embarrassing dreams. I can't get them out of my head."

Notice unexplained changes in behavior. Look for reasons any time your child starts:

- having trouble sleeping.

- acting extremely unhappy about a specific person or place.

- behaving like a much younger child.

- becoming very withdrawn, overly aggressive or irrationally fearful.

- playing adult-sounding sexual games with toys or people.

- having any unexplained physical symptoms such as bruises or inflammation, especially around the genitals or bottom or mouth.

Teaching our children to tell us will help most of the time, but not always. Sometimes children go into denial and block the memory of what happened. They literally make themselves forget. Sometimes children think that, because they didn't follow the rules we gave them, what happened was their fault. They might feel so ashamed that they can't bear to think or talk about it. Our kids need to know that we always want them to tell us, even if it's much later or even if they made a big mistake.

What Should I Do?

If your child says or does something that leads you to fear abuse, it is important to stay very calm. If you become upset, your child's instinct will be to stop saying anything at all. Your child does not want to get into trouble, and might care about and want to protect the abuser. Your child may well want to protect you from the pain that knowing will bring.

Kids live in the here and now more than we do, and the present moment can seem much more important than any past abuse. When I was on a group camping trip, I learned that an eight-year-old girl had been molested several weeks earlier. She told another child that she was willing to talk with me, but not with her parents, even though they were along.

I took the girl, who we'll call Penny, to sit on a log under the trees away from the group. As the sunlight filtered through the branches above us, and the wind played with our hair, Penny explained how it happened. "We played 'truth or dare' and I took the dare. So I felt like I *had* to do what she said. Or I would be breaking my promise." Then Penny added, "Please don't tell my parents."

"Why not?" I asked, knowing that she had a great relationship with them.

"They'll be unhappy, and I don't want to spoil the camping trip." Penny sighed.

"I understand how you feel. But that won't work." I said sympathetically. "I *have* to tell them now. But I'll do my best to explain that you still want to have a fun camping trip."

If you find out that your child might have been molested, expect a flood of outrage, grief, and fear. But these feelings will not serve your child. This is not going to be easy. In a performance worthy of an Academy Award, take a breath, put all your upset feelings aside, and ask your child very calmly, "Why don't you tell me what happened?"

The first thing that you need to say to a child who discloses abuse is something like, "I'm very proud of you for telling me. I know it was hard for you. You didn't do anything wrong. When somebody does something that makes you feel bad, it's not your fault. You are really, really important to me, and we are going to get help."

Next, you need to decide how best to protect this child from further damage. As adults, our job is to take action to make sure that our children are physically and emotionally safe. It's important to act immediately. Seek medical help if necessary. For more serious abuse, it's best to keep your child away from any contact with the abuser until you have some answers. If the abuse is by a family member who is living in the same household, get professional help to figure out what really happened and what needs to be done.

For less serious intrusions, you still need to take action and to monitor the situation. Remember that even apparently "minor" incidents of molestation can have a major impact in a child's life if they are not dealt with. Talk to the people involved. See what their reaction is. Are they concerned about the child or defensive? Are they open to changing their behavior, or are they denying that there's even the slightest possibility that they've done something harmful? Protect your child from any repercussions from the person they told on. Sometimes what seems like a minor molestation is really "the tip of the iceberg" of a much larger problem.

Take care of yourself if you find out that your child has been seriously abused, either sexually or otherwise. It's normal to feel guilty, angry, and betrayed. It's normal to go through a time of being consumed with hate for the person who harmed your child. Painful experiences from your own childhood, which you may have long since dealt with and put aside, are likely to resurface. Seek out the help and support you deserve. As lonely as you may feel, you are not alone.

I have yet to meet a parent anywhere who does not feel guilty about having failed her or his child in some way. The parents, teachers, and other caring adults that I know all do the best that they can for their children. It's hard to accept that even our best is not always enough to prevent assault and abuse from happening to our children. We can give our children the skills to avoid and get out of most bad situations, but not all of them. Even if something goes wrong, we deserve to acknowledge ourselves and our children for the ways in which we did things right.

What if My Child Is Abused by Another Child?

First, follow the same guidelines that are described in the section above. Next, assess whether the abuse was illegal. Overt sexual behavior and serious physical violence should be reported to the appropriate authorities like any other crime. However, much of what we would consider to be damaging behavior is not actually illegal. In any case, you need a plan to ensure your child's physical and emotional safety in the future.

One approach is to help build your child's boundary setting and safety skills. Making up role-plays about the specific situation can be very helpful in understanding how to handle future problems. Work on "reprogramming" any behavior that makes victimization more likely. Consider programs such as Kidpower that give your child the opportunity to practice with other adults and to watch other children using these skills.

It's also important to make sure that the authority figures at schools and other settings your child is in take action to stop abusive behavior. One mother told me, "I want my little girl to stand up for herself more. The little boys pull up her skirt in the kindergarten classroom. It's a game they play with all the girls all the time. Instead of yelling at them, my daughter just cries."

"It's asking a lot of a five-year-old to stand up to behavior that is being tolerated by the people in charge," I pointed out. "The teacher, the yard duty supervisor, and any watching parents should be putting a stop to games like this one. "

You may want to set up a meeting to talk with the people involved in a problem your child is having. This meeting might include the teacher, the other child, the parent of the other child, and/or your child. Be sure to let your child know that you believe what he or she tells you, even if the other child is more articulate. The purpose of the meeting can be to point out the inappropriate behavior and to work out agreements about how to prevent future problems.

Sometimes the best answer is to leave. After her Kidpower workshop, one little girl told her parents that a group of boys had been "humping" her during recess. For several months, they had been playing a game that involved catching her and sandwiching her between them in a very sexual manner. When her parents told the school principal, the playtime was supervised more closely and the boys apologized. However, the mother of one of the boys, who was a volunteer at the school, became very angry. She confronted the little girl and started questioning her about whether she had made the story up. The little girl's parents ended up removing their daughter from the school in order to protect her from further trauma.

If your child has had a traumatic experience caused by another child, make sure that your child gets the emotional support to heal. Counseling can be immensely helpful. It is safest if your child can be protected from further contact with the child who acted as the perpetrator. If separation is not a choice, be aware that it is risky to leave your child unsupervised with the other child.

Take action to make sure that the child who acted as a perpetrator gets help. Be aware that other children in that child's environment might have been abused. The goal is to protect everyone involved from further harm. Taking action may range from a meeting with the child's parents to reporting the situation to authorities.

One Kidpower student, Martin, went on an overnight camping trip with his church group. When the other boy in his tent tried to approach Martin sexually, he shouted, "Get your clothes back on, get in your sleeping bag, and go to sleep!" The boy did what Martin told him to.

The next day, Martin told his mother what happened. She told the church group leader, who suggested calling a meeting of all the parents. Instead, the mother decided to call the mother of the other boy directly. It turned out that this boy was being abused. Through his actions, Martin was able to protect himself and to help another boy get the professional counseling he needed.

What About Reporting Abuse to Authorities?

Laws vary in different states and countries. In most cases, medical, mental health, and educational professionals are required to report suspected child abuse to a government agency such as Social Services or Child Protective Services. It's important to report child abuse even if a case can't be acted upon. Documentation of a prior report can be helpful if another complaint is filed. Remember that other children might also be at risk. Check your local laws and agencies so that you have complete information about what the definition of "suspicion" is and what the definition of "child abuse" is where you live.

It can be frustrating to try to get help for a child. Most agencies are overloaded to the point that they are unable to respond to complaints that are vague and uncertain. Some children live in situations where neglect, emotional attacks, and physical punishment are a daily reality. Even though these experiences are damaging, most of them might be difficult to prosecute legally.

What About Abuse In Families?

Parents and other adults in abusive families need to understand that their actions are damaging to their children. They are likely to have a very poor sense of boundaries, often because they were abused themselves as children. What they are doing seems normal to them rather than abusive. They need to learn what is and is not safe and appropriate to say and do with their children.

Children who are being abused by a family member need a language and a safe place for telling their story. Because children have no basis for comparison, what is happening to them often seems normal to them too. Unless and until they speak up to someone willing and able to take action, it is likely that the abuse will continue. Remember that children who are being abused by the people they love with usually feel love and loyalty for their abuser. They are very likely to believe that the problem is their fault. They do not know how to reach out for help. Many people who have survived terrible incest or physical abuse from their immediate families have told me that they wish they had had Kidpower when they were young. I have wondered how our training would have made a difference. After all, they were children in overwhelmingly destructive homes. They have told me, "Kidpower would have put it into my body that what was happening to me was wrong. I think I would have found someone to help me much, much sooner."

We want to get this message out to children widely without going into the specifics of child abuse. In Kidpower classes, we tell our students, "Sometimes the people kids love have problems. Sometimes these problems are so big that they do things that hurt children or make them feel uncomfortable. If this happens to you or to someone you know, it does not mean that anyone is bad. It does mean, though, that all the people in that situation need help. The way to get help is to find an adult you trust to tell and to keep on telling until somebody does something about it."

One Parting Thought about Sexual Abuse

Although all forms of abuse can be destructive to our children, there is particular shame in our society about sexual abuse. This shame is a large part of the reason why it is so difficult to deal with this issue. It used to be that people believed that, "Only dirty people get head lice." Now we know that head lice can happen to anyone. We take precautions, check for it, and cure it when we find it. If we can learn to deal with sexual abuse the way we have learned to deal with head lice, there will eventually be a lot less of it.

What to do About Bullying

Understand the Problem

Most children will encounter bullying at one time or another. We define bullying as deliberate hurtful or scary behavior from someone close to the child's age and size. Many adults believe that children should work bullying issues out with each other. Yet when they are left to themselves, children are often very confused about what their choices are. Increasingly, studies are showing that children are damaged by bullying behavior—whether they do it, watch it, or are victimized by it.

Bullying behavior—whether it's through threatening words or gestures, physically hurting, name-calling, mimicking, harassing, or shunning—is a destructive force in the lives of too many kids. Being the target of bullying is an attack on a young person's self esteem and joy in life. Doing the bullying causes a child to build behavior that can be destructive socially and professionally later in life. Witnessing bullying creates an upsetting distracting environment in which to play, work and learn.

Bullying is a quick way for individuals or groups to feel powerful or to get attention. Power and attention are strong motivators. Along with finding positive ways of having power and attention, children who bully need the clear message that their destructive behavior is not going to get them what they want.

Make Bullying Against the Rules

Parents need to be clear that bullying is against their family rules. Teachers and school officials need to be clear that bullying is against the school rules. Step in when kids are acting upset with each other in a way that is starting to escalate. Help them learn less destructive ways of handling conflict. Set an example for your child by not allowing people to bully you and by exercising the self-control necessary not to bully others. At home, work at stopping bullying behavior with the same commitment that you would stop someone from throwing all the dishes on the floor and breaking them.

Teach Target Denial

Using target denial will stop most bullies. A fun way to introduce this idea to children is to say dramatically, "There's a *secret* self-defense technique, the *best* technique of all time, which has been handed down from martial artist to martial artist throughout the ages. It's called 'Target Denial,' which means, 'don't be there!'"

To explain further, say, "People who bully want to cause trouble. Good target denial means not being there for that trouble either physically with your body or emotionally with your feelings. You don't want someone's bullying to scare you into being a victim or provoke you into starting a fight. Walking away from someone who is bullying is safer than staying put and getting cornered. Walking away is also safer than escalating a situation by shoving someone out of your way or calling names."

This idea is especially important for teenagers, who sometimes feel that their honor is at stake if they don't have the last word. One of our Kidpower graduates was walking down the street with his friend. Some older boys drove by in a car shouting insults about their mothers. The Kidpower graduate immediately ran into a store to get help. Instead of going with him, the other boy started shouting threats to the boys in the car, who pulled over and beat him up.

What happened in the above story was that the boy who got beaten up was triggered by the insult about his mother. We each have our own triggers or hot buttons. The term "triggers" means language, behavior, or thoughts that cause us to explode with feelings. When our minds are exploding with feelings, it's hard to think clearly and to make wise choices for ourselves.

One way to practice not getting triggered and using Target Denial instead is through what we call the "Have a nice day" or the "No thanks" technique. Pretend to be a bully. Have each child walk past you while you shout age-appropriate insults or threats. Ask the child for ideas on what a bully might say.

The child's job is to walk firmly away from you, look back towards you with a friendly smile, wave a hand, and say something like, "No thanks!" Or, "Bye! Have a nice day! See you later!"—and keep on walking. As the child is leaving shout, "Come back here you wimp!" so that the child can practice looking back one more time while waving and saying, "No thanks!"

When people are trying to pick a fight, it can be very effective to act nice in a sincere way. The child's job is to be calm and centered rather than passive or aggressive. Using a mocking tone of voice or making a sarcastic gesture will be provocative. The best approach is to give a bully *nothing*--neither fear nor anger--to react to.

Like other attackers, bullies go after kids who seem like easy victims. Changing a child's attitude can change what a bully does. A mother told us this story about her nine-year- old son, who we'll call Timmy. "My son has some physical disabilities that make balance and coordination difficult. Several months after Timmy took Kidpower, two boys were suspended from his class for bullying other students. My husband and I were called in by the school counselor. The counselor said the boys had bothered Timmy along with many others. But something was remarkably different about Timmy. Because he was carrying himself in a way in which he looked more confident, he had become much less of a target. I'm sure that's because of what he learned in Kidpower."

Teach Responsibility About Teasing

The most common way people bully each other is through teasing. Kids often don't realize the difference between fun teasing and hurtful teasing. Fun teasing is when everyone involved agrees that it's funny. Fun teasing usually means talking about what someone is good at or doesn't mind being bad at. Teasing becomes hurtful as soon as any one person involved feels like it's not funny. Hurtful teasing usually means talking about what someone has trouble doing or the ways in which someone is different. It's just as important to stop hurtful teasing as it is to stop hurtful hitting.

What seems like a joke to one person can be devastating to another. As one successful professional woman told me, "My childhood was a misery because the other kids made fun of me for being fat. Years later, I found myself in therapy dealing with the pain caused by their laughter."

Finding out what children actually say to each other can be eye opening. A teacher once asked me to come in to her third grade classroom because the teasing had gotten completely out of hand. Too many children were caught up in and getting hurt by the teasing for an idea such as the trash can to work. Of course, the teacher stopped the children when she heard them, but she couldn't be everywhere all the time. She wanted her children to stop themselves.

I started by asking the children, "Well, what is it that you're saying to each other?"

They looked at their teacher to see if answering me was okay. No adult had asked them this question so bluntly before. Then the words came pouring out. It was quickly obvious that this was not language that could be said out loud in an adult's presence in that school without parental permission. Instead, we had the children write the words down.

I still have a file with their misspelled words on smudged torn scraps of paper in childish printing. Curse words. Toilet words. Swear words. Graphic sexual language. Terribly threatening words. Words attacking race, religion, gender, sexual orientation, body size, and body parts. From bright innocent eight-year-olds!

These children were from great homes in an excellent school with a wonderful teacher.

What had started as a game between a few children because of annoyance or boredom had grown into a destructive culture involving the whole classroom. We changed the culture by having children hear stories from adults who had been harmed by the kinds of name-calling that the children were using. By taking the time to address the issue and to help her students understand the consequences of their language, the teacher turned a bad situation into a positive learning experience.

Teach and Use Conflict Resolution Skills

Children who understand and can use conflict resolution skills will be able to prevent most bullying problems. Conflict resolution programs for children and adults teach the following basic concepts and skills:

- Understand that conflict is a normal part of life and that knowing how to resolve conflict is a powerful life skill. Common personal conflicts are about our space, what we say to each other, our property, how we do activities together, and our time.

- Understand the difference between passive, aggressive, and assertive ways of handling conflict.

- Communicate issues through specific respectful "I" messages. For example, "I feel___ _____ (name specific feeling), when you_____ (name specific behavior), Would you please_____ (state exactly what you want the other person to do or not do)."

- Listen respectfully when someone speaks to you. Make sure you understand and that the other person knows that you understand through using active listening, empathic listening, and asking good questions. Respond with your own "I" message.

- Come up with lots of choices that will help resolve the conflict in a way that is respectful to all parties and that gives each person at least part of what he or she wants.

- Think of pros and cons of each choice and come to a mutual decision that both parties will agree to stick with.

- Thank each other for listening and making an agreement.

Some schools even train children to be mediators. My niece was a "Negotiation Buddy" in the second grade. She explained how it works, "When a kid gets mad at another kid, they put their names on the blackboard. It gets very busy because I have a lot of appointments during recess. I take the kid who was mad and the other kid to a quiet place so nobody will bother us. I help the mad kid fill out a card the teacher gave us to have an 'I' message to say what the mad kid feels and wants. The mad kid gives the card to the other kid who says, 'Yes, I will do what you want.' The mad kid isn't mad anymore and says, 'Thank you for listening.'"

"What happens when that doesn't work?" I wondered.

"Then we get the teacher!"

Conflict resolution needs to be backed up by consequences if children break their agreements or get into a pattern of bullying behavior.

Practice Setting Boundaries to Stop Bullying

Most confrontations that involve bullying can be stopped by clear strong boundaries.

Shirley D. Kassebaum, a Counselor at Watson Junior High School, wrote a letter that illustrates this fact. "One of the boys who participated in your workshop used to see me on the average of two or three times a week to complain about someone picking on him. Not long ago, I observed him in the lunch line. The kid in front of him pushed him. He put up his hand and said, in a very loud voice, 'Stop! I don't like to be pushed!'"

To practice, pretend to be a bully, as in the following example.

Bully (strides towards child who is in a corner): "I'm going to get you!" or "Give me your lunch money!"

Child (makes a Stop Sign toward bully's face and yells): "NO! Leave me alone! I mean it!" Next the child disengages and walks away with awareness, calm and confidence.

Self-Defense Against Bullying

As I said earlier, any strong resistance will stop most assaults, including bullying. Often young people won't protect themselves physically from bullying because they don't want to get in trouble at school. Have a frank discussion with children about when it's okay to hurt somebody to stop that person from hurting you. Remind children that physical self-defense should only be used as a last resort, when you cannot leave and you cannot get help. The following bullying self-defense tactics will send a clear physical message, but are unlikely to injure someone:

- strongly pulling away or twisting out of a grab.
- pushing someone out of the way.
- a kick to the shins.
- a punch or hit to the solar plexus to knock the wind out of somebody.
- a pinch to the upper arm or inner thigh to get out of a headlock or grab.

As with any threat, it is always important for children to get help immediately if they have had a confrontation with a bully. In a school environment, reporting what happened to a trustworthy adult as soon as possible can help keep children from getting in trouble with school authorities. Teach children to describe the problem in a regular voice without whining or using blaming language. This makes it easier for adults to understand what happened and to take them seriously.

All of these tactics have been used successfully by Kidpower students. The following story is typical. "Every day at the swimming pool, my 13-year-old daughter was getting dunked under water by an older boy, supposedly in play. When he wouldn't listen to her, she pinched him under the arm. He never dunked her again."

One girl, aged nine, who lives in the inner city, told us, "A bully on the playground grabbed my hair and pulled me backwards. I stopped him by elbowing him once in the stomach. The yard duty teacher complimented me on how I took care of myself without being a bully too. She said she wished she knew how to do that."

Much more often, though, adults tell us that the physical confidence gained from knowing self-defense has been enough for their children to deal with bullies without actually having to fight. One mother told us, "A couple of years ago, my son was injured so badly by bullies that he had to go to the hospital. After that, his victim behavior made him a continual target. Since Kidpower, he has stopped eleven incidents with bullies without ever once having to resort to violence."

Do Not Tolerate Shunning

Martha was the bane of my childhood. Day after day, I'd go to school, dreading recess. All the girls would run to play the wonderful games Martha would lead. If I tried to join in, she'd call them away from me. They'd whisper and giggle and turn their backs. Alone, outside the circle of girls, I'd sit by the door of the classroom and read a book, waiting for recess to be over. Day after day after day.

Shunning happens when a group decides to keep an individual out and to act as if that person is not there. In some cultures, the most devastating punishment anyone could receive was to be shunned. The experience of being banned from the group was life-threatening and sometimes even deadly. The way kids act when they shun others may not seem that serious from our adult perspective, but there have been incidents where children who were shunned committed suicide or acted out in very aggressive ways.

A child being shunned by other children needs our help. Normal boundary-setting skills just don't work. It's too hard to follow our directions to "Just ignore them and play with someone else." It may seem to the child as if everyone important in the world thinks she or he is worthless. This is a time to become actively involved in changing the child's environment. Talk to teachers. Help find new friends. If the situation cannot be resolved, seriously consider changing environments.

Peer Pressure

As young people move into their pre-teen and teen years, the opinions of their peers usually become much more important to them. To make wise decisions, they need to understand the role that peer pressure can play in influencing their choices and have the skills to stand up to their peers when necessary. One excellent resource is the book

How to Say 'No' and Keep your Friends by Sharon Scott. Ms. Scott ran the First Offender program in Dallas, Texas. She found that negative peer pressure was the single most important influence on a young person's decision to break the law. When she taught young offenders tactics for resisting peer pressure, they were far more likely to be successful in staying out of trouble.

Bullying in Schools: Seven Solutions for Parents

Kidpower hears countless stories from upset parents whose children from toddlers to teenagers have been victimized by harassment and bullying at school. School is a big part of our kids' lives but it's usually parents who make the decisions about how and where their children get an education. This means that most young people have no choice about where they go to school.

As parents, we expect schools to provide an environment that is emotionally and physically safe for our children. It's normal to feel terrified and enraged about any kind of threat to our children's well being, especially in a place where they have to be.

Schools are often doing a valiant job of trying to meet an overwhelming array of conflicting demands. But when your own child is being bullied, it is normal for protective parents to want to fix the problem immediately – and maybe to punish the people who caused your child to be hurt, embarrassed or scared.

When possible, try to notice problems when they are small. Pay attention to changes in your child's behavior. Encourage children to tell you about what happens at school. Listen calmly without lecturing. Volunteer even a couple of hours a week in the classroom or school yard so that you can both help out and stay aware of potential problems at school.

If your child has a bullying problem at school, here are seven practical People Safety solutions that can help parents to be effective in taking charge.

1. Stop Yourself From Knee-Jerk Reactions

If your child tells you about being bullied at school, this is an important opportunity for you to model for your child how to be powerful and respectful in solving problems. As hard as it is likely to be, your first job is to calm down. Take a big breath and say, in a quiet and matter-of fact voice, "I'm so glad you're telling me this. I'm sorry this happened to you – please tell me more about exactly what happened so we can figure out what to do. You deserve to feel safe and comfortable at school."

If your child didn't tell you but you found out some other way, say calmly, "I saw this happen/heard about this happening. It looked/sounded like it might be unpleasant for you. Can you tell me more about it?"

If you act upset your child is likely to get upset too. She might want to protect you and herself from your reaction by not telling you about problems in the future or by denying that anything is wrong. The older your child is, the more important it is that she's able to feel some control about any follow-up actions you might take with the school.

In addition, if you act upset when you're approaching school officials or the parents of children who are bothering your child, they're likely to become defensive. Nowadays, school administrators are often fearful of lawsuits, both from the parents of the child who was victimized and from the parents of the child who was accused of causing the problem. This is a real fear because a lawsuit can seriously drain a school's already limited resources.

At the same time, most school administrators truly want to address problems that affect the wellbeing of their students. They're far more likely to respond positively to parents who are approaching them in a calm and respectful way. However, no matter how good a job you do, some people will react badly when they're first told about a problem. Don't let that stop you – stay calm and be persistent about explaining what the issue is and what you want to see happen.

2. **Get Your Facts Right**

Instead of jumping to conclusions or making assumptions, take time to get the whole story. Ask questions of your child in a calm, reassuring way and listen to the answers.

Ask questions of other people who might be involved, making it clear that your goal is to understand and figure out how to address the problem rather than to get even with anybody.

Once you understand the situation, it works best to look for solutions, not for blame. Try to assume that overwhelmed teachers and school administrators deserve support and acknowledgment for what they're doing right as well as to be told what's wrong. Try to assume that children behave in hurtful ways do so because they don't have a better way of meeting their needs or because they have problems in their own lives.

Be your child's advocate, but accept the possibility that your child might have partially provoked or escalated the bullying. You might say, "It's not your fault when someone hurts or makes fun of you, but I am wondering if you can think of another way you might have handled this problem?"

3. **Pinpoint The Cause**

Is the problem caused because the school needs more resources to supervise children properly during recess and lunch, or before and after school? Does your child need to learn skills for self-protection and boundary-setting by making and practicing a plan with you or by taking a class such as Kidpower? Does the school need help formulating a clear policy that makes behavior that threatens, hurts, scares, or embarrasses others against the rules? Does the child who harmed your child need help too?

4. **Protect Your Child**

Your highest priority is, of course, to protect your child as best you can. Try to step back for perspective and keep the big picture in mind as well as the immediate problem. What protecting your child means will vary depending on the ability of the school to resolve the problem, the nature of the problem, and on the specific needs of your child.

Through a programs such as Kidpower, make sure your child has the chance to practice skills in order to walk away from people who being rude or threatening, to protect himself or herself emotionally and physically, and to ask for help sooner rather than later.

In some cases, protecting your child might mean that her teacher and school principal, the parents of the other child, and you all work on a plan together to stop the problem. In other cases, the best solution for your child might be to change schools.

In extreme cases, you might want to explore legal action. Different countries and states have different laws about children's rights. If need be, explore the resources available in your community.

5. **Prevent Future Problems**

You also want to prevent future problems. All children deserve to be in an environment that is emotionally and physically safe. Dealing with ongoing harassment is like living with pollution – eventually, coping with the constant assault can undermine your child's health.

Concerned parents can help schools find and implement age-appropriate programs that create a culture of respect, caring, and safety between young people rather than of competition, harassment, and disregard.

6. **Get Help For Your Child**

Finally, you want to get help for your child and for yourself to deal with the feelings that result from having had an upsetting experience. Sometimes bullying can remind you about bad experiences in your own past. Parents often have to deal with guilt for not preventing the problem, and sometimes struggle with rage.

Getting help might mean talking issues over with other supportive adults who can listen to you and your child with perspective and compassion. Getting help might mean going to a therapist or talking with counselors provided by the school or by other agencies.

7. Make This Into A Learning Experience

As parents, it's normal to want to protect our children from all harm. If we monitor their lives so closely that they never fall, never fail, and never get hurt or sad, then we'd be depriving our children of having the room to grow.

Upsetting experiences don't have to lead to long-term damage if children are listened to respectfully, if the problem is resolved, and if their feelings are supported. Young people can take charge of their safety by learning skills for preventing and stopping harassment themselves, by setting boundaries, avoiding people whose behavior is problematic, and getting help when they need it.

Working with Different Age Groups

The skills of self-protection and confidence are the same whether we are three or one hundred and three. What changes at different ages are the contexts in which we use these skills, and some of our abilities.

What if My Child is Just Learning to Talk?

Even before children can speak well enough to understand and practice the safety rules, there is a great deal you can do. Lay a groundwork to give your children the confidence and self-esteem they need to be able to keep themselves safe. Make sure that the people who care for your children treat their bodies with respect. Give them many opportunities to learn how to make decisions by letting them choose in situations that are appropriate — for example, whether to have milk or juice, walk or be carried, read a book or go to the park.

Most importantly, make sure that young children in your life get to choose whether or not they are touched for the purposes of affection and play and whether or not they are teased. This may mean that you have to stop other adults from hugging, kissing, teasing, or tickling them.

Make sure that a toddler is never left alone in the yard or the store or the car or the bath, even "for just a second." Trust your instincts and check out any suspicious behavior or negative reactions your child has to someone, even if the person is someone you really like and respect.

Play in ways that build safety skills. For example, sometimes change the game where you pretend to be a monster and you say, "I'm going to get you!" The child says 'No, you're not!' and giggles and runs away. Usually, that game ends with the adult catching the child yelling, "I GOTCHA!" Instead, teach your child to turn around and yell 'NO!' with a stop sign and have the monster run away whimpering.

More Freedom = More Responsibility

The older our children get, the more confusing it gets to be a parent. When do we stand firm? When do we let go? How do we find a balance between taking responsibility for keeping our children safe and helping them to develop their own sense of responsibility and independence?

Author Richard Riera, Ph.D., in his wonderful book *Uncommon Sense for Parents with Teenagers*, says that when our children are young, we are the managers of their lives. Part of their developmental process as they grow older is to fire us as managers so that they can become the managers of their own lives. Our job is to allow ourselves to be fired gracefully but not too soon as managers, and then to do our best to get hired back as consultants.

This means that as children become older and more independent, sooner or later, the adults in their lives must allow them to have more freedom. To feel safe doing this, we want our children to show us that they have the awareness to recognize potentially dangerous situations and the skills to get out of these situations when necessary. Many parents have made participation in Kidpower or Teenpower workshops a requirement of relaxing their restrictions.

Look for situations in which your older children can take over the job of managing their lives. Within the guidelines you set, encourage them to organize their own schedules, make their own appointments, earn their own money, select their own clothes, prepare their own food, and pay for things themselves. Give them the responsibility of doing their part to help your household run smoothly.

Keep having conversations about what makes different situations safe or unsafe. For example, an older child might go alone to a public bathroom and even say hello to another person there. But suppose that this person started trying to touch the child or started asking personal questions like, "Are you here alone?" Or, "Where do you live?" The child's safety plan would then be to leave the bathroom right away.

As young people become more independent, you will need to keep negotiating about what your rules are and why. For young people who seem to need to define themselves in opposition to you, acknowledge the value of their drive to be independent even while holding your ground. For shyer or more compliant children, find ways to notice and reinforce assertive behavior. For example, find occasions to say, "You really did a good job of letting me know what you thought."

Older children appreciate being told the truth. "We can make sure that you understand our expectations about taking care of your well-being and safety, but we can't control your choices when we're not there. It will be up to you to decide at the time how best to handle a situation."

Being Advocates for Our Children

Building Communities of Safety

As adults, we need to take responsibility for ensuring that our children's environments are as safe as possible. At home, this means having good locks on the doors and windows, good lighting and visibility around the house, and easy access to a telephone in different rooms. When we drive, it means keeping our car doors locked. Sometimes people resent having to live this way. They want to believe that their communities and homes are always safe.

Criminals take advantage of this wish. Police officers tell us that most home robberies are not break-ins at all, but walk-ins. The grandmother of a young girl who was kidnapped by a man who walked into the house through an unlocked door put it like this, "If you had a precious diamond ring, would you leave it lying around for anyone to pick up? Our children are far more precious than any diamond. Yet our denial keeps us from being as careful with our children as we would be with our jewelry."

At school or in other settings where we leave our children, it's our job to be sure that there is adequate supervision. I have heard numerous stories of children just wandering away from the playground. Sometimes it takes hours before anyone notices they're missing.

We need to insist that discipline problems be handled. I have heard stories about children being terrorized even in very good schools.

When we notice potentially dangerous situations, we owe it to our children to speak up. Dealing with the resistance of large impersonal systems and overwhelmed people in positions of authority can leave us feeling helpless and hopeless. The truth is that even one dedicated person can make a lasting difference.

For example, in 1989, one mother, Molly Wetzel, founded the Safe Streets Now program to help neighborhoods fight drug use. This nonprofit organization teaches groups of neighbors to work together to bring pressure on landlords to evict drug-dealing tenants. Ms. Wetzel's crusade began when her 17-year-old daughter was harassed by drug users on a street right next to their home. As a result of her determination, her neighborhood in West Berkeley became a much safer place and she inspired people all over the country to turn their neighborhoods around.

Pay Attention

Molesters gravitate toward activities that involve children. On the surface, they can be extremely charming, kind people. Parents and teachers need to keep continual awareness about the potential for abuse and take care not to trust someone alone with children just on superficial appearances or credentials.

In San Jose, a man representing himself as a doctor went to a child care center. He told the teacher that he was sent by the County to inspect some of the children and showed her some official-looking papers verifying this. He took different children into a room alone and molested them. One little girl knew enough to tell her teacher that she was uncomfortable with how "the doctor" had touched her. Although extremely upset that she had allowed something like this to happen in her center, the teacher alerted authorities, and they were able to catch the man when he went to another center.

Speak Out

Once our children come to us and tell us that they are uncomfortable with somebody, or once we notice a problem ourselves, we must act. To do otherwise because of our own discomfort in facing confrontations is to betray the trust of our children. We want our children to speak up for themselves, and we have to set the example by speaking up for them.

When my daughter was twelve, her advanced math teacher kept looking at her in a leering way and making suggestive remarks. She said, "I feel uncomfortable when you talk about how I look. Please don't do that." In response, he did it more.

Although she didn't like the idea, I persuaded my daughter that it was important for me to tell her teacher that what he was doing was not okay, not only for her sake, but for the three other girls in her class as well as the boys who were watching this teacher.

I made an appointment to meet the math teacher after school and said very respectfully, "I think you're an excellent teacher. You may not be aware of some things you're doing which make my daughter uncomfortable. I feel that your teasing remarks about how she looks are just not appropriate."

The teacher, who was a large man, seemed to get bigger and bigger and redder and redder in the face as I was talking, until he exploded, "In my thirty-two years of teaching, no one has ever spoken to me like this!"

"Well," I said cheerfully, "after thirty-two years, it's probably about time."

"Get real!" he snapped. "Your daughter needs to stop being over sensitive when someone just makes a joke! Anyway, who are *you* to talk to *me* like this?"

I'm her MOTHER, I thought, and the Co-Founder of Kidpower! But what I said in a firm quiet voice was, "There are probably women right now who are sitting in a therapist's office saying that they stopped studying math or other subjects important to them because of that kind of 'just jokes.' What you're doing is a form of sexual harassment, and I want you to stop. If need be, we can ask the school counselor to help us understand each other."

In the face of this adult version of "Stop or I'll tell," the math teacher deflated like a pricked balloon. "I'll do whatever you want! " he said, and then added plaintively, "But I feel bad because your daughter doesn't like me!"

I sighed. "She might if you'd stop teasing her! However, it's not her job to like you, and it's not your job to like her. It's your job to teach her math, and it's her job to learn it."

After that, the math teacher's behavior changed, and my daughter did well in the class.

When approaching someone with a problem, it's important to stay calm and focused. Most people do not realize that their behavior is inappropriate and uncomfortable for another person. They may respond defensively because accepting the results of their behavior forces them to change. The most effective way to prevent getting caught up in someone else's defensive reaction is stay very clear ourselves.

If someone we are close to is upset by what we say, we might need to spend some time acknowledging feelings. Many conflict resolution models for boundary-setting emphasize listening compassionately to someone's perspective as a first step towards helping that person become ready to hear our reasons for insisting on a change. If you need to raise an issue that you know will be emotionally difficult, you might want to practice ahead of time. Your goal is to avoid getting triggered into reacting defensively yourself instead of communicating that you care while sticking to your point.

A major issue for kids at school is that, if they are in a fight, the rule usually is that both students will be suspended no matter who is at fault. Maria, a bilingual aide, told us this story. "After trying unsuccessfully for months to stop the sexual harassment my thirteen-year-old daughter was enduring from a couple of boys, I enrolled her in Kidpower and wrote her school a letter saying that I would back her up if she needed to protect herself. When one of the worst offenders grabbed her, she knocked the wind out of him. Not only did all of the boys treat her with respect after that, but the school developed a policy on sexual harassment."

Even if we can't make a situation better right away, it is important for our kids to know we take them seriously, and that we are doing whatever we can to fix the problem.

Helping Our Children Feel Empowered in the Face of Armed Violence in Schools

Right after the shootings at Columbine High School, a six-year-old girl in a workshop at a private school asked me, "What if someone comes to our school and starts shooting everybody?" Along with all of the other adults in the room, I looked into her little face and felt ill that she even had to wonder about it.

The issue of armed violence in schools becomes heart-breakingly and urgently on our minds each time a new tragedy takes place. The threat of violence looms over all children no matter where they live or what their family situation is. It is important to address the concerns of children as gun violence is occurring more frequently and is ever-present in the media. Although nothing works all of the time, the following suggestions can help children to feel less helpless and more prepared.

Be a Safe Calm Person to Talk To

Children of any age need to know that adults are willing to listen to their fears. It is important that adults treat children with respect when they talk about their problems. You need to find a balance between listening and supporting without burdening children with your own fears.

Because of your own anxieties, it might be tempting to try to make children feel better in the moment by pretending that the situation is not really that bad. If you act like something is too terrifying even to talk about, this will make children more afraid. They might want to protect you by not sharing their fears and this can leave them feeling really alone.

It can also be hard not to overreact and sound panic-stricken yourself. If their adults are overwhelmed and afraid, it can be traumatic for children.

Children need adults to listen and explain what is happening and what they should do as calmly and matter-of-factly as possible. Tell children to tell you if *anyone* is making them uncomfortable about *anything*. Having children get into the habit of talking to you will help you to judge whether or not a situation is potentially dangerous.

Make Sure It Is Safe to Tell at School

It is your job as an adult to take charge of the environments in which your children spend time as best you can. Make sure that your school has a plan for dealing with armed violence just like any other emergency. Make sure that adults are trained in how to deal with a child who makes a report about another child. One girl who was in a very exclusive school in a quiet neighborhood heard a boy bragging about his gun. When she told the principal, the gun was found and the boy was suspended. However, the principal handled the situation in a way that caused the girl to be identified and then he put her back into the classroom. The boy's friends threatened to kill her. The trauma she went through could have been prevented if the school officials had understood how important it was to protect the girl's identity.

What Adults Can Say to Children About What Happens to People's Minds and Bodies in an Emergency

You can tell children, "Any time you have an emergency--like a car wreck, an earthquake, a flood, a tornado, or somebody being dangerous-- your first feeling will most likely be disbelief. You will probably think, 'It's not true. It is impossible! This can't be!' The sooner you can get over your disbelief and see what is actually happening, the sooner you can start to protect yourself."

"Next, you will probably experience some very strong feelings because of a chemical in your body called adrenaline. Adrenaline can make you feel full of energy, or it can make you feel shaky, weak or sick to your stomach. Sometimes all of these feelings come at the same time, which can be a bit confusing. Your body might go into a panic and want to run or freeze or start fighting, whether it makes sense or not. The *good news* is that you can learn to use the energy from your adrenaline to give you *lots of power* while still thinking clearly so you can make the safest choices for yourself. If you practice the safest way to handle different emergencies, you will be able to act quickly because your body will already know what to do."

Rehearsing how to handle different emergencies through role plays can prepare children to react effectively and quickly -- and to have their adrenaline work for them instead of against them.

What Adults Can Say to Children About Getting Away, Getting Hurt, and Getting Help

Most children want to know what to do if the worst happens. It is less upsetting to imagine a plan than to keep imagining disaster. You can tell children, "The safest thing to do almost always if someone starts waving a gun or a knife or starts shooting is to get away as quickly and quietly as you can. You will almost always be safer if you keep running away even if the person with the gun tells you to stop. Even if the person is saying he or she will hurt someone else if you run, the best chance you have for helping that person is to run away and get help."

It is good for children to have a safety plan for how to get out of a building in case of danger – whether the danger comes from a fire or a person. You can say, "Your job is to get out of the building as far from the danger as possible. So let's think about everywhere you might be and how you might get out if you need to. You can go out the door or, if you have to, jump out of the window. If you cannot get out and the danger is from a fire, look for a place near a window, away from the fire and yell for help. If the danger is from a person and you cannot get out, look for a place to hide that covers up all of you."

It is worth getting injured to get away from someone who is shooting. One of the boys at Columbine escaped by throwing himself out the window. He got cut up badly but he survived and is having a good life. Most of the children who were standing still in shock or who were hiding under the tables got shot.

You can tell children who are worried about this, "You might need to get hurt in order to get away. If a gun shoots, it will be loud. The great thing about adrenaline is that it can help you to run fast, even if you are hurt or start to bleed. If you are hurt by a gun, you can get better most of the time, just like you get better most of the time when you fall down and get hurt and bloody."

Tell children, "Once you get out, as soon as you safely can, find an adult you trust to go to for help. Now, let's think about different places you might be and where you could go to get help after you got out." Take the time to brainstorm ideas about getting out and getting help with the children. Teach children how to call 911; their full name, address, and telephone number; and how to use different types of telephones.

What If Kids Bring Weapons to School?

You can tell children that, "Sometimes kids like to joke or brag about having or using guns or bombs or about hurting animals or people. Most of the time, they are just pretending, but once in a while, they are not. If someone is talking like this, this person might have big problems and I want you to tell me about it as soon as you can."

If someone is showing off having a weapon, children need to know how to get away without saying what they think. This might mean that they have to lie to stay safe and say, "Of course I won't tell." Or even, "Yes, I think that's cool." They might have to agree with the person who is being weird or scary, even with a big insult like saying, "Yes, you're right, my mom is a creep (or worse)."

It is urgent that, if someone is acting in a way that could be dangerous, children go to an adult they trust and say something like, "This is about my safety and about the safety of others here at our school. I need you to promise to protect me from other people knowing that I am the one who is telling you this. I want you to call my parents (or another safe adult) right away so they can be with me."

If children don't feel safe with any adult at school, it is important that they tell their parents or another safe adult as soon as they can. The school needs to know if there is possible danger. In some situations it may be necessary to make a telephone call to the school anonymously--which means not telling your name--to someone in charge, like the principal. Anonymous telephone calls or notes will only be taken seriously if there are as many specifics as possible included in the message.

Practicing Leaving

If children are really worried about somebody shooting at school, or any other kind of emergency, practicing can help them manage that worry. In the private school workshop that I mentioned at the beginning, when the little girl asked her question about someone shooting at school, the anxiety in the room was huge. All of the children, and their teachers and parents, were looking at me, needing an answer.

I said, "Television makes it seem as if scary things like this are happening all the time. But this isn't true. Most of us will live long happy lives and never have to worry about somebody starting to shoot people at school. But it is good to know what to do in an emergency. Most of the time, the safest thing you can do is leave quickly and quietly when someone is acting violent. Just get up and get out. Suppose that I started acting dangerous. Look around and see if you know how to get out of this room.... now, all of you, very quietly leave the room."

Thirty children found one of the three exits and silently streamed outside to their teachers who were waiting for them outside. Then they all came back and we went on with our workshop.

Think about the Underlying Issues

In order to create long-term change, each of us needs to find our own ways of helping to address the underlying issues that lead to school violence. Important actions can include:

- Establishing school policies that make violence, threats, and harassment against the rules with clearly defined consequences.

- Providing education and policies to stop prejudice, bullying, and harassment.

- Mentoring a troubled child;

- Monitoring and being aware of the ways in which television, video games, music, the Internet, and movies normalize violence for children.

- Educating school personnel, law enforcement officials, and parents about warning signals.

- Making sure that school counseling is available to families whose children show signals of problems as early in their lives as possible.

- Helping young people learn conflict resolution, self-protection, boundary-setting, and confidence skills through organizing and supporting programs such as Kidpower.

Develop a School Violence and Harassment Prevention Policy

Kidpower recommends that all schools have a clear written policy statement that describes the school's commitment and procedures for addressing issues of violence and harassment. This written statement should be sent home at the beginning of the school year with a letter to parents which includes recommendations for how to talk with their children about the rules. Please feel free to adapt the following sample policy from Kidpower to fit the needs of your school.

Sample School Violence and Harassment Prevention Policy

Our commitment is to ensuring an emotionally and physically safe environment in our school community. We will do our best to stop any behavior which is threatening, harassing, bullying, or dangerous. If any student, parent, or staff member feels threatened, upset, or endangered by someone's behavior, that person has both the right and the responsibility to speak up.

Our goal is to prevent problems whenever possible. We offer conflict resolution training and self protection and boundary-setting training through our school community. We ask parents to discuss our expectations with their children. Even young children can be told, "We expect you to be safe at school. If anything ever happens that makes you feel unsafe or unhappy, we want you to go to a teacher for help right away and to tell us as soon as you can. We also expect you to act in ways which are safe and respectful to other people. If you or the school tells us that you have threatened or been disrespectful to someone, we will work together to help you figure out how to solve problems with people in other ways." Even though we cannot make our children feel safe all the time, it is important that they get in the habit of talking problems over with their parents and teachers. If they feel worried or unsafe, we don't want them to feel alone and we do want them to have adult help in figuring out what to do.

If a problem occurs, our focus is on addressing situations in ways which seek solutions rather than blame. We will do our best to deal with problems in a fair and effective fashion.

Most concerns about student behavior can be resolved at the classroom level by talking with the teacher or by speaking directly with the individuals involved. If this doesn't work or if a serious incident occurs, the following process will take place.

1. The teacher and the parents of the child or children involved will meet with the principal and school counselor. A plan will be made so that students will understand what went wrong and will get the counseling or other support they need to prevent future problems. Every effort will be made to protect students raising concerns from retaliation.

2. A letter will go home to parents in the classroom without naming the families involved. The letter will describe what happened and what steps were taken to address the situation. The letter will suggest how parents might talk with their children about what happened in an age-appropriate positive way.

3. For a severe situation, a meeting will be held so parents can discuss their concerns and get help in how to talk to their children.

4. Where appropriate, training will be offered to the parents, teachers, and students involved in the incident.

If there is a concern involving the behavior of an adult working at the school, most of the time this concern can be resolved by speaking directly with that individual. If this doesn't work, or if the incident is too severe, the principal or school counselor should be approached with the problem. A plan will be set up to resolve the situation in a solution-oriented, fair, and respectful fashion for everyone involved.

Fact Sheet About Kidpower®

What is Kidpower Teenpower Fullpower International®?
Kidpower Teenpower Fullpower International (shortened to Kidpower) is a charitable educational nonprofit organization founded in Santa Cruz, California in 1989. Our vision is to work together to create cultures of caring, respect, and safety for everyone, everywhere. Our mission is to teach people of all ages and abilities, especially children in need, to use their power to stay safe, act wisely, and believe in themselves.

Experts highly recommend the Kidpower method for being positive, practical, and relevant for children, teenagers, and adults from many different cultures. Worldwide, we have served over two million people, including those with special needs, through educational resources, in-person workshops, curriculum development, and consulting.

Why is Kidpower Important?
The "People Safety" skills taught by Kidpower prepare individuals to be safe with others and with themselves. Our society promotes the importance of Fire Safety skills, for example, not only to avoid getting hurt by fire, but also to be able to enjoy the use of fire for cooking, for warmth, and for fun. This is why we call this set of skills "Fire Safety" rather than just "Burning Prevention."

People Safety skills include: boundaries to develop better relationships; safety plans to prepare for the unexpected; advocacy skills to speak up for the emotional and physical well-being of oneself and others; self-protection strategies to prevent most trouble before it starts; and self-defense skills to stop emergencies. These skills can prevent most bullying, harassment, molestation, assault, and abduction. Even though the issues can be serious, the Kidpower approach is empowering, dynamic, and fun.

What Resources Does Kidpower Offer?
Kidpower offers workshops, publications, and training that all incorporate our very positive and effective method of teaching People Safety skills. Our teaching method includes:
- Explanation of important concepts through examples that are meaningful and age-appropriate for our participants;
- Activities designed to give each student the opportunity for successful practice of each skill presented; and
- Adaptation to be relevant to the life-situations, cultures, and abilities of different individuals.

We provide a wealth of free information through our online Library at **Kidpower.org** in the form of articles, enewsletters, videos, and podcasts In addition, we provide consultation by email to individuals around the world about how to use our People Safety skills to address specific problems.

How Did Kidpower Begin?
In collaboration with many other committed people, Executive Director/Founder Irene van der Zande has led the development of services, training of instructors and organization of centers since our organization was established in 1989. The incident that inspired Irene happened in 1985 in Santa Cruz, California when she protected 8 young children, including her 7-year-old daughter and her 4-year-old son, from a man who was threatening to kidnap them. Irene gathered educators, law enforcement officials, mental health professionals, martial artists, safety experts, and parents to start Kidpower, which evolved into Kidpower Teenpower Fullpower International.

Who Else is Involved in Kidpower?
Ellen Bass, co-author of the groundbreaking book *The Courage to Heal: A Guide for Women Survivors of Childhood Sexual Abuse*, is the Founding President of our Board of Directors. Timothy Dunphy, a sixth degree Black Belt and international champion winner in Taekwondo, is our Program Co-Founder. Hundreds of highly dedicated people teach our programs, organize our workshops, lead our Centers, and serve on our Boards of Directors. These individuals are leaders in their own communities. They include social workers, attorneys, therapists, martial artists, educators, physicians, police officers, community organizers, and business people. They include friends, parents, other family members, neighbors, and employers.

What Programs Are Offered?
Everyday Safety Training provides practices designed to prepare students to be safe every day with people they know, peers, bullies, and strangers. Full Force Training offers students the opportunity to practice self-defense skills full force with a head-to-toe padded instructor.

Workshops include: Kidpower for children from 3 to 12 and their parents, teachers, or caregivers; Teenpower for teenagers; Fullpower for adults; Workpower for work place safety programs; Collegepower for college students; Parentpower to help parents and caregivers set boundaries, manage emotions, and get help; and Seniorpower for older people. We also offer Adapted Programs for people with difficult life challenges such as having a disability, living in a dangerous place, or being a survivor of violence and abuse.

Professional Staff Training for schools and agencies serving youths and adults prepare their staff to teach People Safety skills on their own and to incorporate our system of teaching into their own curriculum or activities. Teacherpower provides nonviolent aggression management skills to professional educators. Our Reaching Out Project prepares professionals working with charitable organizations in countries that have great economic challenges to teach People Safety skills to youth and adults in dangerous life situations.

Is There Any Proof That Kidpower is Effective?

For years, we have had very positive evaluations and feedback from our participants, including many success stories of people using their personal safety skills both to improve their daily lives and to stop dangerous situations.

In 2004, the effectiveness of our services for young children was documented through an outside professional evaluation of our Kidpower program conducted by LaFrance Associates with funding from the Lucile Packard Foundation for Children's Health. Almost 95% of the parents and caregivers of over 550 Head Start children from multicultural low-income families observed that their children were safer because of their Kidpower training. Parents and caregivers reported that most of these 3 to 5-year-old children remembered most of the skills four to nine months after the training. Over 90% reported that they personally felt better prepared to explain safety skills to their children.

In 2005, a similar study was conducted by an independent professional evaluator with 840 8 to 12-year-old students and their teachers in New Zealand. Both teachers and children reported after three months that the students used the skills to reduce conflict, that learning the skills increased their confidence and reduced their anxiety, and that they found that the program was "fun." In 2002, a research project for a PhD study on the effects of self-protection training of early adolescent girls trained by Kidpower and another organization found that Kidpower has all of the elements that the girls defined as being important for their training to help them both feel and be safer.

In 2010, thanks to a grant from the Ruddie Memorial Youth Foundation, the firm of Shattuck Applied Research and Evaluation conducted a study on a population of 238 third-grade children in Santa Cruz County that presents evidence of effectiveness of the Kidpower Everyday Safety Skills Program. The researcher utilized a quasi-experimental, time series research design with a matched comparison group. The Kidpower school-based workshop and follow up "booster" sessions were designed to help youth build self-esteem and learn how to prevent bullying, harassment, and violence, thus reducing the risk of victimization and lessening their likelihood of becoming perpetrators during their lifetimes.

The findings demonstrated that the two-hour training and reinforcement activities positively contributed to an immediate increase in children's safety knowledge and that the effect was retained three months after the workshop. The findings demonstrated that children in the treatment group increased their safety skills knowledge in seven core competency areas that were not present in the study's control group. These results supported our hypothesis that children's safety knowledge was enhanced significantly by the Kidpower Everyday Safety Skills program. This study extends the evidence that Kidpower's school-based safety skills program can enhance protective factors associated with preventing and stopping most bullying, molestation, violence, and abduction.

Kidpower Educational Publications

The Kidpower Book for Caring Adults: Personal Safety, Self-Protection, Confidence, and Advocacy for Young People provides an in-depth explanation of the Kidpower method for preparing young people to protect their emotional and physical safety and to speak up effectively for themselves and others. Through inspiring stories, clear explanations, and step-by-step directions, the reader learns how to assess personal safety concerns for the young people in their lives and make realistic plans; teach personal safety skills to prevent most bullying, sexual abuse, assault, and abduction; use boundary-setting and advocacy skills to build better relationships; and bring personal safety skills and ideas to children, youth, and teens with difficult life challenges.

Bullying: What Adults Need to Know and Do to Keep Kids Safe provides curriculum being used by many families, schools, and youth organizations for their own anti-bullying activities.

The Kidpower Safety Comics for Adults With Younger Children is a cartoon-illustrated tool to help adults introduce People Safety skills to children from three- to ten-years-old who are usually with adult caregivers. However, the skills are important for people of any age – adults too! Older children often learn by reading and practicing with younger children. The humorous cartoons illustrate social stories to discuss with children. Directions for adults introduce how to practice skills that can prepare children to protect their emotional and physical well-being. Available both in English and in a bilingual English and Spanish version.

We also have our *Kidpower Safety Comics for Older Children*. The tools in this book are most appropriate for youth ages nine to thirteen who are becoming more independent.

The Kidpower Teaching Kit is a set of five cartoon-illustrated handbooks with social stories and lesson plans for introducing personal skills in classrooms and other group settings. The focus is on children ages three to eight, but is relevant for any children up to age ten, who are not out on their own. Books include: Safety with Feelings and Words, Being Powerful to be Safe (including Safety with Cars), Safety with Touch and Teasing, Getting Help to be Safe, and Checking First. to be Safe (includes Safety with Strangers). Available both in English and a bilingual English and Spanish version.

The Fullpower Safety Plan Comic Book is a cartoon-illustrated introduction to personal safety skills for teens and adults in simple language. The humorous black-and-white drawings provide an entertaining explanation of basic skills that can protect people's emotional and physical safety most of the time. The simple explanations and clear drawings were first designed for people with developmental delays or whose first language is not English. However, the concepts and skills are relevant to teens or adults regardless of their abilities from a wide range of cultures around the world.

The Fullpower Teaching Kit is a set of six manuals using cartoons, entertaining stories, and simple language to prepare teachers to introduce and practice personal safety with teens and adults. This information can help people of different abilities and cultures to protect themselves from most bullying, molestation, assault and abduction.

Kidpower® Services for All Ages and Abilities

Kidpower of Colorado

Kidpower of Colorado was established in 1994 and has taught more than 35,000 children and adults the skills and self-confidence that they need to stay safe. Kidpower was established locally by Jan Isaacs Henry and Jan DeBoer, both practicing psychotherapists, and Debra Campeau, an attorney guardian ad litem, whose collective experience with individuals dealing with trauma underscored the need for early intervention for children.

Kidpower offers comprehensive safety education programs in several formats: school and agency classes, Weekend Family workshops (ages 7-12), Starting Strong workshops (ages 4-6), Teenpower violence prevention workshops, counselor/teacher training, and customized workshops designed to accommodate special needs of participants. Community education presentations teach people about the importance and effectiveness of safety education in a variety of settings. Kidpower values collaboration and is proud to have partnered with 200 other agencies, organizations and schools in Colorado.

Free On-Line Library. Our extensive on-line Library offers over 100 free "People Safety" resources including articles, videos, webinars, blog entries, and podcasts. We regularly send new resources directly to our subscribers through our Kidpower News and Bullying Solutions e-newsletters. Free downloads are available of our Kidpower® International Safety Signs, our Kidpower® 30-Skill Challenge, a coloring book, and most articles. In addition, we give permission to organizations, blogs, and media sources to use and share these materials without cost for charitable purposes that meet our criteria.

Coaching, Consulting, and Curriculum Development. Long-distance coaching by video-conferencing, telephone, and e-mail enables us to make our services accessible worldwide. We consult with organizations and schools on how to best adapt our program to meet their needs and develop new curriculum to increase the "People Safety" knowledge of different groups facing difficult life challenges.

Workshops. Through our active centers and travelling instructors, Kidpower has conducted workshops in over 40 countries spanning six continents. Our programs include: Kidpower Parent/Caregiver Education seminars; Parent-Child workshops; Weekend Family Workshops; classroom and teacher training programs; Teenpower self-defense workshops for teens; CollegePower for young people leaving home; Fullpower self-defense and boundary-setting workshops for adults; SeniorPower for older people; programs for people with special needs; training for professionals; and workplace violence prevention and communication programs.

Instructor Training and Center Development. Our very comprehensive training program prepares qualified people to teach our programs and to establish centers and offices for organizing services in their communities under our organizational umbrella.

About the Author

Irene van der Zande is the Executive Director and Founder of Kidpower Teenpower Fullpower International. Since 1989, she has led the development of the programs, training of instructors, and establishment of new Centers. Irene has taught self-protection and confidence-building workshops for thousands of children, teenagers, and adults. She is an expert at designing programs to help people facing special life challenges.

Irene is also the author of *The Kidpower Book for Caring Adults, Bullying: What Adults Need to Know and Do to Keep Kids Safe*, the *Comprehensive Program Manuals* for training instructors, the cartoon-illustrated materials, and numerous articles about using People Safety skills in daily life for people of all ages and abilities.

Prior to starting Kidpower, Irene wrote a book called *1,2,3 . . . The Toddler Years* that is used in early childhood education programs in colleges all over the United States. She is also the co-author of *Parent/Toddler Groups: A Model for Effective Intervention to Facilitate Normal Growth and Development,* published by the Early Childhood Center of the Cedars-Sinai Medical Center.

Kidpower has been a gift of love to the world from Irene and her family as well as from hundreds of other dedicated people. Her husband, Ed, donates much of his time to write grants to help support the organization. Their two children, Chantal and Arend, are now adults who have grown up along with Kidpower.

Acknowledgements

In this Colorado edition of our Kidpower Guide, I want to acknowledge the amazing leadership, commitment, integrity, and talent of Center Director Jan Isaacs Henry and all of our Colorado instructors, board members, students, sponsoring schools and organizations, and supporters. Together you have brought training to over 35,000 people and protected countless children through sharing Kidpower knowledge widely in your state. I also want to thank Jan for her many contributions to Kidpower Teenpower Fullpower International. I feel honored to have her as a friend, Senior Program Leader, and mentor in this work.

The thought, creativity, and experience of many different people over many different years are incorporated into this book. Timothy Dunphy, Co-Founder of the Kidpower program and a Sixth-degree Blackbelt in Taekwondo, has contributed heavily to the development of the Kidpower program. Timothy's partnership, wisdom, and support have been essential to our success every step of the way. Our curriculum and organization has been greatly enhanced at all levels by the insight and expertise of Joe Connelly, who is our Great Lakes Regional Director and a Seventh Degree Blackbelt in Taekwondo. Founding Board President Ellen Bass has contributed years of uncommon sense and faith just when it's been needed the most.

Many thanks, in no particular order and representing the tip of the iceberg, to:

Jerilyn Munyon, Susan Wilde, and Sheryll Doran for their role in the Kidpower pilot program development; Dr. Sherryll Kraizer for the contributions her Safe Child Program has made to our teachings for younger children; Marsha Kearns for the Kidpower name; David Keip for fresh insight and the yappy dog story; Carol Middleton for her strength, vision, and inspiration through the years; Steve and Lea Sassone for dedication and warmth and Sonoma County; Eve Bertrandias for lunches, tea, and friendship; Mark Morris for helping me find the right tools for managing conflict, merging on the freeway, and training people in self-defense; Ken Regelson for building our first bridge to the blind community, for making Colorado happen, and for a lifetime of brotherhood; Jean Glowacki for leadership with 4-H and the Colorado front range community; Ann Mason for quiet strength;Peter Alsop for putting our work into song and for balance; Cornelia Baumgartner for building our national collaboration with the New Zealand Police, her creativity in creating new resources, and for dedicated leadership in New Zealand; Erika Leonard for her tremendous commitment, talent and creativity and leadership in California;Kim Leisey for years of leadership in the Washington D.C. area and, with Nancy Young, for Collegepower; Martin Hartman for years of commitment in New Zealand; Joe Ferrando for his huge heart and deep commitment; David Harrison, M.D., for leadership in Vancouver and with our padded instructor training; Mark Meilleur for years of dedication in Quebec; Raim Regelson for teaching me to walk in as if I own the place and a lifetime of fatherhood; Marylaine Leger for her incredible leadership in Montreal and with the Reaching Out Conference; Beth McGreevy for bringing us into the 21st Century on the World Wide Web and into public view with marketing; Lily Regelson for teaching me to tune in to others and for a lifetime of motherhood;

Annette Washington for being an oasis of peace and love and power in a crowded world; Janice Flynn for unwavering commitment to our getting to the next level as an organization and her leadership on the Board; Elaine Regelson for management wisdom and being our first donor ever and for our lifelong sisterhood; Claire Laughlin for saying "I'll do anything to help"—and meaning it!; Arnie Kamrin for his great heart, generosity and great contacts; Peter Lewis, Ph.D. for building bridges to the independent school community; John Luna-Sparks, LCSW, for his incredible passion for helping those who are most vulnerable feel and be safe; Abbie Bleistein, M.D., for her dedication as a Board member and for leadership in bringing Kidpower to her community;Karen Ho for being a monthly donor for over 15 years and for years of exceptional support; Nancy Driscoll for her leadership on the Board, generosity, and great spirit; Jan Isaacs Henry for having coffee together by telephone and e-mail and the wonderful resources she keeps bringing to our work.

Also, thank you to Sudiep Biddle, Claire Laughlin, Elaine Regelson, Eugene Tanner, Shmuel Thaler, and Pat West for photographs and to Chantal Keeney for drawings.

All of the remarkable people who lead our Centers, teach our programs, serve on our board, work in our offices, donate, organize workshops, and volunteer provide the foundation for our programs. The experiences and ideas from our students of all ages and abilities continually enrich our creativity and understanding. Thanks to the dedication of everyone—old and new—the Kidpower community of leaders and programs keeps growing and getting better.

I want to express appreciation to our Board of Directors and Senior Program Leaders for their years of encouragement, generosity, commitment, and friendship. These talented people are working with great commitment and determination to move Kidpower forward so that we will be able to realize our potential as an organization.

To the Board members and supporters of our centers from around the world, I want to thank you for your generosity and commitment in bringing Kidpower services to your communities.

Drawing by a 10 year-old after participating in a KIDPOWER workshop

Made in the USA
San Bernardino, CA
20 June 2015